clay-pot
cooking

clay-pot
cooking

slow-cooked casseroles, tagines and stews

jennie shapter

southwater

This edition is published by Southwater

Southwater is an imprint of Anness Publishing Ltd, Hermes House, 88–89 Blackfriars Road, London SE1 8HA
tel. 020 7401 2077; fax 020 7633 9499; www.southwaterbooks.com; info@anness.com
© Anness Publishing Ltd 2003

UK agent: The Manning Partnership Ltd, 6 The Old Dairy, Melcombe Road, Bath BA2 3LR
tel. 01225 478444; fax 01225 478440; sales@manning-partnership.co.uk
UK distributor: Grantham Book Services Ltd, Isaac Newton Way, Alma Park Industrial Estate, Grantham, Lincs NG31 9SD
tel. 01476 541080; fax 01476 541061; orders@gbs.tbs-ltd.co.uk
North American agent/distributor: National Book Network, 4501 Forbes Boulevard, Suite 200, Lanham, MD 20706
tel. 301 459 3366; fax 301 429 5746; www.nbnbooks.com
Australian agent/distributor: Pan Macmillan Australia, Level 18, St Martins Tower, 31 Market St, Sydney, NSW 2000
tel. 1300 135 113; fax 1300 135 103; customer.service@macmillan.com.au
New Zealand agent/distributor: David Bateman Ltd, 30 Tarndale Grove, Off Bush Road, Albany, Auckland
tel. (09) 415 7664; fax (09) 415 8892

A CIP catalogue record for this book is available from the British Library.

Publisher: Joanna Lorenz
Managing Editor: Linda Fraser
Project Editor: Laura Seber
Production Controller: Darren Price
Designer: Nigel Partridge
Jacket Design: Balley Design
Photography: James Duncan, Ian Garlick, Michelle Garrett, Amanda Heywood, David Jordan, Dave King,
William Lingwood, Patrick McLeavey, Thomas Odulate, Craig Robertson, Sam Stowell
Recipes: Alex Barker, Michelle Berriedale-Johnson, Kit Chan, Jacqueline Clarke, Matthew Drennan, Sarah Edmonds,
Joanna Farrow, Brian Glover, Nicola Graimes, Christine Ingram, Lucy Knox, Lesley Mackley, Sally Mansfield,
Sallie Morris, Jennie Shapter, Anne Sheasby, Steven Wheeler, Kate Whiteman, Jeni Wright

Previously published as part of a larger compendium, *The One-pot and Clay-pot Cookbook*

NOTES
Bracketed terms are intended for American readers.

For all recipes, quantities are given in both metric and imperial measures and, where appropriate, measures are also given in
standard cups and spoons. Follow one set, but not a mixture because they are not interchangeable.
Standard spoon and cup measures are level. 1 tsp = 5ml, 1 tbsp = 15ml, 1 cup = 250ml/8fl oz

Australian standard tablespoons are 20ml. Australian readers should use 3 tsp in place of
1 tbsp for measuring small quantities of gelatine, flour, salt etc.

Medium (US large) eggs are used unless otherwise stated.

1 3 5 7 9 10 8 6 4 2

CONTENTS

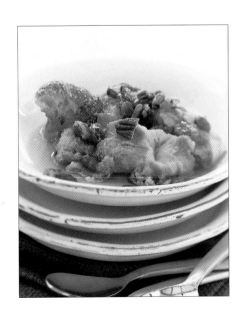

INTRODUCTION

There's nothing new about cooking in clay. Thousands of years ago, hunters discovered that coating small birds and animals in clay before baking them in an open fire kept the meat juicy and prevented it from burning. Any feathers or spines would come away easily with the clay, leaving just the tender, edible part. But getting damp clay every time one wanted to cook was somewhat time-consuming and often impossible. Reusable clay pots, therefore, were a huge improvement, and this material was used by many of the ancient civilizations. Today, clay pots based on ancient designs are still widely used all over the world. In North Africa, it is the conical tagine; in China, the sand pot; in Spain, the cazuela; and in France, the daubière and tian.

A moist method of cooking

Clay pots are not the same as ordinary bakeware: they are left unglazed, which means that they are porous. The clay container is soaked in water before cooking and, as the container heats up, the water turns to steam, keeping the contents beautifully moist and tender. The only other liquid comes from the food itself, so the full flavour of the food can be appreciated. Because this ancient form of cooking seals in all the food's natural juices, it ensures that vitamins and minerals are retained, and since it requires very little or no fat, it is extremely healthy. Clay pots also retain heat well, so if you need to prepare dinner in advance, the food will stay hot. This makes this style of cooking perfect for everyone, from students to families.

Above: Creating dishes in individual earthenware pots makes them easy to serve – and leaves less crockery to wash.

Left: The tall, conical tagine from north Africa is one of the many ancient clay pot designs that are still widely used today.

Below: A whole chicken cooked with vegetables and herbs makes the perfect pot-roast and needs little attention once it is in the oven.

transform them into tasty pie fillings, simply by sandwiching them inside ready-rolled puff pastry or filo.

Chicken bricks, bean pots, tians and tagines come in all shapes and sizes. Some must be used in the oven; but others can be used on top of the stove and some can even be used in the microwave. They need to be treated kindly, but are surprisingly durable. If you've never used one – or have forgotten just how good they make food taste – this book will give you plenty of inspiration. Whether cooking for the family, a dinner party, or simply a light meal for one, you will soon discover just how easy clay pot cooking can be – with delicious results.

Left: Clay pots come in a whole host of sizes and shapes. These tiny shallow cazuelas can be used to bake individual portions of both savoury and sweet tarts, roasted vegetables and custards.

Versatile and easy to use

Elaborate dinner parties are a rarity these days. On the menu instead are simple dishes prepared with the minimum of fuss but with maximum flavour. Clay pot stews, casseroles, hot-pots and curries are easy to prepare, a pleasure to serve and the perfect choice for family and friends. They require a minimal amount of preparation and so the cook can relax, secure in the knowledge that there will be no last-minute sauces to make, no tricky toppings to produce. Serving a selection of side dishes is unnecessary when vegetables are included anyway, so you have the perfect excuse for offering only the simplest accompaniments, sparing yourself the anxiety that comes with trying to get everything ready at precisely the same time. These dishes tend to be fairly good-natured, and will seldom spoil if not eaten the moment they are ready. Some, like curries and casseroles, actually improve if made the day before, so that all the flavours can bed down together and blend.

Clay pot dishes are not limited to casseroles and stews, however. You can also cook fish, poultry and joints whole,

create pies, tarts and soufflés, roast vegetables, make soups, risottos and paellas, and even whip up desserts. There's very little washing up, and if there are any leftovers from casseroles or stews, you may well be able to

Below: A fully glazed clay pot is the ideal container for this contemporary twist on a traditional Italian frittata. The glazing ensures that the flavours don't soak into the pot, which means that it can be used for both sweet and savoury dishes.

CLAY-POT EQUIPMENT

Visit any market in any town the world over, and you will find clay cooking pots for sale. Some will be rough, rustic items, only suitable for display, but others – like the Spanish cazuela or the North African tagine – will be intended not for the tourist trade, but for everyday cooking. Before buying, always seek local advice as to the durability and safety of the items, especially as regards any glazes that might be used. Buying a boxed item from a reputable store may not be as romantic, but it is probably more sensible. Clay cooking pots need special treatment, and it makes sense to follow the instructions that come with your particular utensil.

Romertopfs

Perhaps the most familiar unglazed clay pots are those produced by Romertopf. Their extensive range includes items suitable for cooking meat, fish, vegetables, fruit, even bread and cakes. The classic Romertopf is a rectangular pot with a deep, wide base and a domed lid. These come in several sizes. Other shapes include a long oval, suitable for accommodating a whole fish. This has a glazed base, to prevent liquid from penetrating the porous clay and leaving behind a lingering fishy smell.

Left: The classic, high, domed Romertopf dish (top) and a large oval clay pot that is especially designed for cooking whole fish.

Lids are designed to fit snugly, so that they cannot accidentally slip off, but there is a narrow gap between the lid and the base that allows any excess steam to escape from the clay pot.

Right: This deep, pan-shaped clay pot is designed for cooking bean dishes, but would also be good for baking potatoes, and for cooking soups and stews that have lots of liquid.

Above: The shape of these deep-based clay pots makes them ideal for baking potatoes and cooking beans and pulses.

Bean Pot/Potato Brick

There are several shapes of these deep, round pots. Some have a handle for easy lifting. Made entirely from clay, the pots have a domed lid. Although these pots are especially suitable for slowly cooking beans and pulses, they can also be used for soups and stews, and the shape is ideal for cooking both large and small potatoes. The potatoes are bathed in a layer of steam, which keeps them moist during cooking.

Whatever you are cooking, the pot and lid should first be soaked in water, then placed in a cold oven after the ingredients have been added.

If you are cooking beans, check the recipe or the manufacturer's handbook. Before being added to the pot, such varieties as kidney, cannellini and soya beans need to be brought to the boil in a pan of water, then boiled vigorously for about 10 minutes to eliminate toxins from the beans. Drain the beans and leave them to cool before adding them to the bean pot. Any liquid added to the pot should be cold. This will prevent the pot from cracking or breaking.

Garlic Baker

This small terracotta dish with a domed lid is used for baking garlic. Like all clay pots, it must be placed in a cold oven and heated gradually. There is no need

Above: This large chicken brick is designed to hold a whole bird.

to soak the pot in water first. The inside of the dish is glazed, so the garlic juices will not permeate it. The baker will accommodate four to six garlic bulbs. A small cross must be cut in the top of each garlic bulb, or the tops can be sliced off, to prevent them from bursting during cooking. The steam they release will be trapped under the domed lid of the garlic baker, and will keep the garlic cloves beautifully moist and tender. The garlic baker can also be used in a microwave oven.

Onion Baker

This clay pot looks like a larger version of the garlic baker. It consists of a shallow terracotta dish with a high, domed lid; it will accommodate four medium-sized onions, and can also be used for cooking onion wedges, shallots or baby onions. The lid can be soaked in water first, so that it releases steam during cooking. The steam helps to tenderize the onions. Towards the end of cooking, the lid should be removed so that the onions turn brown and become caramelized.

Chicken Brick

This is a large, unglazed fire clay cooking dish with a high lid. The largest ones are designed to hold a whole chicken, guinea fowl or duck, but can also be used to cook any large piece of meat or poultry. Smaller chicken bricks are ideal for small birds and portions. There is no need to add fat or liquid to the pot unless the recipe specifically requires this.

Above: The onion baker (left) and the garlic baker both have high, domed lids that are designed to trap steam during cooking.

Chinese Sand Pot

This covered earthenware pot, which is sometimes called a Chinese casserole, is usually glazed on the inside only and reinforced on the outside with wire. It comes from China, where it was originally used to cook stews over a slow charcoal fire. Several shapes and sizes are available. They are not expensive and can be bought in Asian and Chinese food and cooking equipment stores. The sand pot is ideal for slow-cooked dishes such as soups and stews that are baked in the oven. Do not use sand pots on top of the stove unless the manufacturer recommends this. Sand pots are fairly fragile, and are prone to crack easily. They do not need to be soaked before baking but like other clay pots are best placed in a cold oven.

Tagine

This North African cooking pot consists of a large, shallow base and a tall, conical lid. The dish that is cooked in it is also known as a tagine.

Left: *The Chinese sand pot was designed for cooking over a slow charcoal fire, but it is equally at home in a modern oven.*

Above: *The traditional tagine (above left) has a shallow base and a tall, conical lid, while the contemporary version (right) has a deeper, larger base.*

The food is placed in the base. As it cooks, steam rises and is trapped in the lid, keeping the food moist. Tagines are traditionally made from glazed brown earthenware, sometimes with a slightly rounded base. They come in a range of sizes, from small individual tagines to family-size ones that measure at least 20cm/8in across. There is also a modern version, with a heavy, cast-iron base and a glazed earthenware lid. Unlike the traditional tagine, which can only be used in the oven, or on a barbecue whose coals have been dowsed with sand, this design can also be used on top of the stove. This is very convenient, since it means that onions, vegetables and other ingredients such as meat and poultry can be browned in the base before the lid is fitted and the tagine is placed in the oven. Some glazed earthenware tagines can be used on top of the stove on a low heat, but it is best to use a heat diffuser; always check the manufacturer's instructions.

WHAT'S IN A NAME?

Clay, earthenware, terracotta, stoneware – we use the terms interchangeably, but are they all the same thing? Clay is essentially the raw material; it is a fine-grained mix of mineral origin that occurs in sedimentary rocks and soils. It is malleable when moist, but hardens when it is heated. When pots that are made from clay are baked, they become earthenware.

Terracotta is an Italian word that means "baked earth". It has come to refer to a type of hard, brownish-red earthenware that is traditionally left unglazed.

Stoneware is stronger than earthenware, having been fired at a higher temperature. It is usually perfectly safe to put stoneware in a hot oven, but always check the manufacturer's instructions.

Cazuelas

These shallow, lidless earthenware dishes originated in Spain. They are made in a variety of sizes. The smallest, suitable for Catalan-style sweet custards, measure 10–12.5cm/4–5in across, while the largest – used for cooking savoury dishes in the oven – measure 38cm/15in or even more. They vary in depth from about 2.5cm/1in to 7.5cm/3in. Cazuelas are either partially glazed on the outside, and fully glazed inside, or glazed inside and out. Neither type are soaked in water before use. After a while, the glaze on the cazuela may develop a slightly "crazed" appearance, but this is completely natural and will not affect the performance of the dish.

Individual cazuelas can be used for cooking single portions of all sorts of one-pot dishes, but they are ideal for making individual upside-down tarts. The lightly fried vegetables are spread out on the cazuelas, topped with rounds of puff pastry, then baked in the oven. The tarts are then inverted on serving plates.

Left: Spanish cazuelas come in a range of sizes and depths. The smallest are perfect for individual oven-baked custards, while the largest are good for slow-cooked stews and vegetable bakes, but will also accommodate whole fish and poultry as well as large joints of meat.

Tian

This traditional French baking dish originated in Provence. It is a shallow, usually oval, earthenware dish, and is used for baking vegetables, sometimes with rice and eggs. The dish that is cooked in it is also called a tian.

Right: Oval-shaped tians originated in Provence and are traditionally used for baking vegetables, but the shape is ideal for other oven-baked, one-pot dishes.

Glazed Earthenware Bakeware

A wide selection of glazed ovenproof earthenware is available. These dishes can often be put straight into a hot oven, or used under a hot grill (broiler) for browning. They are also suitable for use in the freezer. Unlike clay pots and porous earthenware, they do not need to be soaked in water before use and will not absorb food flavours and become tainted.

Right: A wide range of glazed earthenware bakeware is available – these dishes can often be used in the oven and under the grill.

CLAY-POT COOKING TECHNIQUES

Used with care, clay cooking pots last for years, but it is very important to follow the manufacturer's instructions closely. The advice that follows should be read in conjunction with your handbook.

Preparing a Clay Pot
All unglazed clay cooking pots must be soaked in cold water before every use. This is essential because it is the water retained in the clay that provides the moisture required during cooking. Ideally, the soaking time should be about 20 minutes. If it is the first time you have used the pot, leave it to soak for at least 30 minutes.

Place both the pot and its lid in a sink of cold water, inverting the lid on top of the base if necessary. The entire pot and the lid must be submerged. This thorough soaking is recommended before every use. If you are really short of time, you can just hold the pot under cold running water for about 1 minute, but this is not as satisfactory as soaking.

You can use your clay pot for lots of different recipes, but should avoid cooking fish or any highly flavoured dish in it the first time you use it. If you have more than one clay pot, consider keeping separate pots for savoury and sweet dishes.

Partially Glazed Clay Pots
Also available are clay pots that are glazed on the inside, but which have unglazed lids. With this type of pot, only the lid needs to be soaked, and this is done by holding it under running cold water for a few minutes. The ingredients are put into the pot, seasoned, and moistened with stock. The lid is fitted

and the pot is placed in a cold oven, which is then heated to 220°C/425°F/Gas 7. Steam released from the soaked lid helps to keep the food moist as it bakes. The lid can be removed towards the end of cooking to allow the food to brown, if necessary.

Cooking with a Clay Pot
Most clay pots should only be used in the oven. Unglazed pots are sensitive to sudden changes of temperature, which can cause the pot to crack or break if it is placed directly over the heat.

Some clay pots can be used on top of the stove on a very low heat, but it is recommended that a heat diffuser or flame-tamer is used. These are available from specialist cookware stores.

1 Some recipes suggest sautéing vegetables or meat in a frying pan to brown them before adding them to the clay pot. If you do this, let the browned foods cool slightly before putting them into the cold clay pot.

2 Once the browned foods have been added, it is okay to pour in warm or hand-hot cooking liquids. If what is in the pot is cold, any liquid added should be at room temperature.

USING A HEAT DIFFUSER

If your handbook states that your pot can safely be used on top of the stove you can obviously do so, but always use a heat diffuser between the heat source and the pot.

Some cazuelas can be used on top of the stove with a heat diffuser.

Cooking in an Oven
An unglazed clay pot must always be heated gradually.

Place the clay pot in a cold oven and then heat to the required temperature. It might crack if subjected to a sudden change of temperature.

You will notice that the recipes in this book advise you to place the clay pot, which will be cold, in a cold oven, then set the oven temperature to allow the oven and clay pot to heat slowly.

An electric oven heats up gradually, giving the clay pot time to acclimatize. If, however, you are using a traditional gas oven, the flames may be too fierce for the cold clay pot. You should start by setting the oven temperature to 190°C/375°F/Gas 5. After 5 minutes, increase the temperature to 200°C/400°F/Gas 6. Continue to increase the temperature of the oven gradually, each time raising it to the next setting on your cooker, until the required temperature is reached.

The exact cooking times for recipes containing liquids may vary from oven to oven, as the time taken for the liquid to come to the boil will differ.

Cooking with a Cast-iron Tagine on a Stovetop
In addition to the classic all-earthenware tagines, which can't be used on a stovetop, there is a modern version that has an earthenware lid and cast-iron base. The base can be used on the top of any type of stove, be it gas, electric or wood-burning, to brown ingredients such as onions, vegetables or meat before the other ingredients and liquid are added. The pot is then covered and the tagine or stew is simmered gently on top of the stove or in the oven.

Place the cast-iron tagine base on the stovetop, add a little oil and heat. Add the vegetables or other ingredients and cook over a medium-high heat, stirring occasionally, until browned

Browning in a Clay Pot
A certain amount of browning will occur during cooking, depending on the cooking temperature, cooking time and type of food. Some recipes suggest removing the lid for a short period of time towards the end of the cooking time to enhance the colour of baked items and roasts, and also to develop a crisper finish. The oven temperature for clay-pot cooking is fairly high, so the browning process will only take a few minutes; keep a close check on the food.

To remove the lid, lift the clay pot out of the oven using oven gloves and place it on a pot stand, wooden board or folded dishtowel. Take care when lifting the lid to avoid any escaping steam.

Adding Liquids to a Clay Pot
Never add boiling liquids – or even very hot liquids – to a cold clay pot or the sudden change in temperature may cause the claypot to crack.

If you need to add liquid to the clay pot during the cooking period, this liquid should be hot. This not only avoids a sudden temperature change, but also ensures that the food isn't cooled too much, which would slow the cooking.

Adding Flavourings

To get the best results, place herb sprigs and spices in among vegetables that are to be roasted or underneath joints of meat. This will ensure that the flavour penetrates as deeply as possible.

Adding Ingredients during Cooking
In some recipes, ingredients that don't need to be cooked for long, such as prawns or cooked ham, are added towards the end of the cooking time.

Remove the pot from the oven using oven gloves and remove the lid. Add the cold food and stir well to ensure that it is distributed evenly, then re-cover the pot and return it to the oven.

Cooking on a Barbecue
Moroccan tagines are sometimes placed on a barbecue, but they should not be too near the heat source. It is best to wait until the coals have all turned grey. Cover the coals with some sand, to make the heat less concentrated, and then allow the tagine to heat up slowly by initially placing it at the edge of the barbecue and gradually moving it to the hottest part.

Using a Clay Pot for Baking

Clay pots can be used for baking cakes, breads and sponge-based desserts. It is, however, best to keep a separate clay pot for sweet foods or, alternatively, use earthenware that is glazed inside.

If you use a clay pot for baking, it is a good idea to line the base of the clay pot with a piece of baking parchment, so that the food doesn't stick to the base and is easy to remove after baking.

SAFETY FIRST

When you remove any type of clay pot from the oven, either to add extra ingredients or to serve the food, protect your hands with oven gloves. Place the pot on a folded towel, wooden board, heatproof mat or pot stand, as sudden contact with a cold surface could cause the pot to crack. Do the same with the lid, when you lift it off.

Clay pots should not be used under the grill (broiler) or in the freezer as the sudden change in temperature could cause the clay pot to crack or break.

Microwave Cooking

Clay pots can be used to cook foods in the microwave oven, as well as in a conventional oven. One of the advantages with using a clay pot for microwave cooking is that, because it is moist from soaking, it will absorb some of the microwave energy. This slows down the cooking process, which is perfect for protecting delicate foods, cooking foods more evenly and pot-roasting less tender cuts of meat, whole chickens or game birds.

Select a clay pot that will fit inside your microwave oven. The smaller, rectangular or round pots are ideal.

Prepare the pot as for oven cooking, by soaking it in water for 20 minutes. When setting the cooking time, refer to your microwave handbook for detailed instructions on using a clay pot, as each appliance is different. If you are adapting an existing microwave recipe, expect the food to take slightly longer to cook in a clay pot. The food is usually cooked on full (100%) power, but it may also be cooked on medium-high (70%) or medium (50%) settings so that the food simmers, rather than boils.

A safety note worth remembering is that because a clay pot is moist and absorbs microwave energy it will become hot; hotter, in fact, than many other types of microwave cookware. Make sure you use oven gloves to lift the clay pot out of the microwave, and always place the pot on a pot stand, wooden board or mat, or folded dishtowel when removing it from the oven, both for your own safety, and to avoid subjecting the pot to severe temperature changes.

ADAPTING RECIPES FOR CLAY-POT COOKING

A wide range of foods can be cooked in a clay pot, and you may wish to try using it for some of your favourite dishes. Find a clay-pot recipe in this book that is similar to the one you want to make, and use it as a blueprint. The main differences in cooking techniques that need to be observed are these:

• When an unglazed or partially glazed clay pot is used, the oven must not be preheated.

• When the pot is put into the cold oven, it is heated gradually until it reaches the required cooking temperature. If the dish contains liquid, it must be heated until it boils. This is likely to be at a higher temperature than when cooking in another type of container, because the pot forms an insulating layer between the heat of the oven and the food. When the liquid boils, the oven temperature may then be reduced, so that the contents of the pot simmer.

• If you are using a gas stove, it is essential that you increase the temperature gradually or the transition from cold to blasting heat may cause the pot to crack.

• You will probably have to extend the cooking time to take into account the fact that the ingredients, including any liquids, are cold when put into the oven, which also starts off cold. When foods are roasted with little or no liquid, however, the cooking time stays about the same because the higher cooking temperature compensates for the insulation of the clay pot.

• Because of the moist environment, food cooked in a clay pot doesn't overcook quickly when the lid is on, however, it is important to check the food frequently if the lid is removed towards the end of cooking to promote browning as the top of the food can easily scorch.

Cleaning and Storing Clay Pots

Before using a clay pot for the first time, brush it thoroughly inside and out to remove any loose clay particles left from the manufacturing process. Rinse the pot after brushing, then drain it. If you intend to cook in it straight away, then soak it thoroughly in cold water first.

After using the pot a few times, you may notice a colour change. This is completely natural and is part of the character of a clay pot. As with a well-seasoned frying pan or wok, this effect is due to a protective layer that builds up with use and enhances the cooking qualities of the pot.

Washing the Pot

1 Wash a clay pot promptly after every use, using a brush and hot water. A soft-bristled brush is fine if the pot is not too dirty, otherwise use a firm-bristled washing-up brush, Add washing-up liquid to the water if this is recommended in your handbook, as this helps to get rid of stubborn stains. Avoid using abrasive cleaning materials as detergents, as these may affect the porous nature of the clay and may impair its cooking qualities.

2 Having washed the pot, rinse it under hot water, then stand it upside down on kitchen paper to drain thoroughly.

Using a Dishwasher

Most glazed earthenware dishes can be used in the dishwasher, but some manufacturers do not recommend washing clay pots that way. Check your manufacturer's handbook.

Removing Food Residue

Sometimes food may bake on to the surface of a clay pot, especially if it has been used for cooking without the cover. Soaking the pot in hot water to which a little washing-up liquid has been added is usually sufficient to release the residue. Leave the pot to soak overnight if the residue is particularly stubborn. Some earthenware dishes can be filled with hot water to remove baked-on food, but do not leave them immersed in hot soapy water.

1 If an unglazed clay pot becomes tainted with residual flavours, soak it overnight in cold water containing bicarbonate of soda (baking soda). If the problem is severe, or if smells still linger, fill the pot with water, add bicarbonate of soda and place it in a cold oven.

2 Set the oven to 180°C/350°F/Gas 4 and leave the clay pot to heat in the oven for about 20 minutes. Increase the temperature of the oven to 200°C/400°F/Gas 6 and heat for another 20 minutes, then increase the oven temperature again to 230°C/450°F/Gas 8 and leave the pot at this temperature for 30 minutes to 1 hour.

3 Carefully lift the pot out of the oven using oven gloves and then discard the contents. Scrub the interior of the pot gently before rinsing it thoroughly with very hot water. Turn the pot and lid upside-down on a rack and leave to dry at room temperature. It is worth following this cleaning procedure after about a hundred uses, to clean the pores of your clay pot. This will allow it to take up water with the same efficiency as when it was brand new.

Storing the Pot

Before you put a clay pot away, make sure that it is not only completely clean but also thoroughly dried.

Invert the lid into the base. This is not only for safety and so that it takes up less room in your storecupboard, but also because placing the lid on the pot as for cooking could encourage moulds and mildew to grow on the inside surface of the pot and lid.

It is for this reason that the pot must also be stored somewhere dry and airy. Do not leave it in a damp place. It is the nature of a clay pot to absorb moisture, so it is important to keep it completely dry during storage. Do not wrap the clay pot or seal it in a plastic bag during storage.

FIRST COURSES AND LIGHT MEALS

When you are cooking a first course, appetizer

or snack for family or friends, the most

successful dishes are often the simplest,

so anything that can be cooked in a clay pot is a

sure winner. Whether you opt for soup, soufflés

or seafood, or try your hand at a hot and spicy

clay-pot treat such as Potato Wedges with

Tomato and Chilli Salsa, everyone will be glad

you chose the easy option.

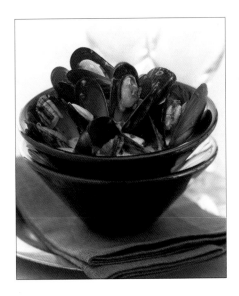

CHINESE CHICKEN and CHILLI SOUP

Ginger and lemon grass add an aromatic note to this tasty, refreshing soup, which can be served as a light lunch or appetizer.

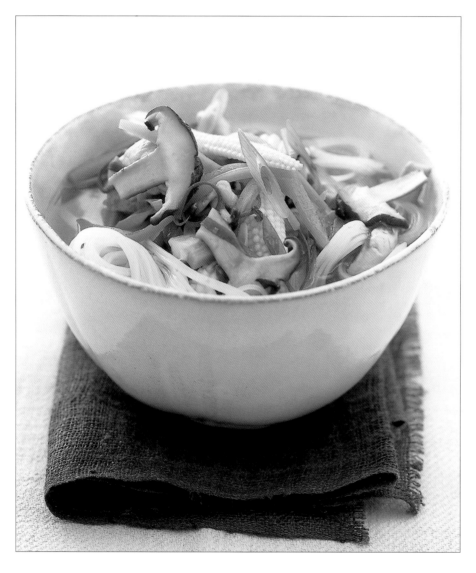

SERVES 4

150g/5oz boneless chicken breast portion, cut into thin strips
2.5cm/1in piece fresh root ginger, finely chopped
5cm/2in piece lemon grass stalk, finely chopped
1 red chilli, seeded and thinly sliced
8 baby corn cobs, halved lengthwise
1 large carrot, cut into thin sticks
1 litre/1¾ pints/4 cups hot chicken stock
4 spring onions (scallions), thinly sliced
12 small shiitake mushrooms, sliced
115g/4oz/1 cup vermicelli rice noodles
30ml/2 tbsp soy sauce
salt and ground black pepper

1 Place the chicken strips, chopped ginger, chopped lemon grass and sliced chilli in a Chinese sand pot. Add the halved baby corn and the carrot sticks. Pour over the hot chicken stock and cover the pot.

2 Place the Chinese sand pot in an unheated oven. Set the temperature to 200°C/400°F/Gas 6 and cook the soup for 30–40 minutes, or until the stock is simmering and the chicken and vegetables are tender.

3 Add the spring onions and mushrooms, cover and return the pot to the oven for 10 minutes. Meanwhile place the noodles in a large bowl and cover with boiling water – soak for the required time, following the packet instructions.

4 Drain the noodles and divide among four warmed serving bowls. Stir the soy sauce into the soup and season with salt and pepper. Divide the soup between the bowls and serve immediately.

COOK'S TIP
Rice noodles are available in a variety of thicknesses and can be bought in straight lengths or in coils or loops. They are a creamy white colour and very brittle in texture. Rice noodles are pre-cooked so they only require a very short soaking time – check the packet for exact timings. Vermicelli rice noodles are very fine and will only need to be soaked for a few minutes.

BEAN and PISTOU SOUP

This hearty vegetarian soup is a typical Provençal-style soup, richly flavoured with a home-made garlic and fresh basil pistou sauce.

SERVES 4–6

150g/5oz/scant 1 cup dried haricot (navy)
    beans, soaked overnight in cold water
150g/5oz/scant 1 cup dried flageolet or
    cannellini beans, soaked overnight in
    cold water
1 onion, chopped
1.2 litres/2 pints/5 cups hot vegetable stock
2 carrots, roughly chopped
225g/8oz Savoy cabbage, shredded
1 large potato, about 225g/8oz,
    roughly chopped
225g/8oz French (green) beans, chopped
salt and ground black pepper
basil leaves, to garnish

For the pistou
4 garlic cloves
8 large sprigs basil leaves
90ml/6 tbsp olive oil
60ml/4 tbsp freshly grated
    Parmesan cheese

3 Add the chopped carrots, shredded cabbage, chopped potato and French beans to the bean pot. Season with salt and pepper, cover and return the pot to the oven. Reduce the oven temperature to 180°C/350°F/Gas 4 and cook for 1 hour, or until all the vegetables are cooked right through.

4 Meanwhile place the garlic and basil in a mortar and pound with a pestle, then gradually beat in the oil. Stir in the grated Parmesan. Stir half the pistou into the soup and then ladle into warmed soup bowls. Top each bowl of soup with a spoonful of the remaining pistou and serve garnished with basil.

1 Soak a bean pot in cold water for 20 minutes then drain. Drain the soaked haricot and flageolet or cannellini beans and place in the bean pot. Add the chopped onion and pour over sufficient cold water to come 5cm/2in above the beans. Cover and place the pot in an unheated oven. Set the oven to 200°C/400°F/Gas 6 and cook for about 1½ hours, or until the beans are tender.

2 Drain the beans and onions. Place half the beans and onions in a food processor or blender and process to a paste. Return the drained beans and the bean paste to the bean pot. Add the hot vegetable stock.

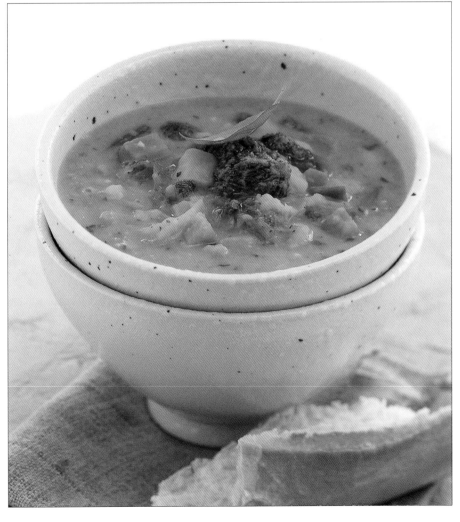

OVEN-ROASTED RED ONIONS

The wonderful taste of these sweet red onions is enhanced still further with the powerful flavours of fresh rosemary and juniper berries, and the added tangy sweetness from the balsamic vinegar.

SERVES 4

4 large or 8 small red onions
45ml/3 tbsp olive oil
6 juniper berries, crushed
8 small rosemary sprigs
30ml/2 tbsp balsamic vinegar
salt and ground black pepper

VARIATION
Add a similar quantity of long, thin potato wedges to the onion. Use a larger dish so that the vegetables are still in one layer.

COOK'S TIP
To help hold back the tears during preparation, chill the onions first for about 30 minutes and then remove the root end last. The root contains the largest concentration of the sulphuric compounds that make the eyes water.

1 Soak a clay onion baker in cold water for 15 minutes, then drain. If the base of the baker is glazed, only the lid will need to be soaked.

2 Trim the roots from the onions and remove the skins, if you like. Cut the onions from the tip to the root, cutting the large onions into quarters and the small onions in half.

3 Rub the onions with olive oil, salt and pepper and the juniper berries. Place the onions in the baker, inserting the rosemary in among the onions. Pour the remaining olive oil and vinegar over.

4 Cover and place in an unheated oven. Set the oven to 200°C/400°F/Gas 6 and cook for 40 minutes. Remove the lid and cook for a further 10 minutes.

WILD MUSHROOM and SUN-DRIED TOMATO SOUFFLES

These impressive little soufflés are baked in individual earthenware pots. They are packed with rich, Italian flavours and are remarkably easy to prepare and cook.

SERVES 4

25g/1oz/½ cup dried cep mushrooms
40g/1½oz/3 tbsp butter, plus extra
   for greasing
20ml/4 tsp grated Parmesan cheese
40g/1½oz/⅓ cup plain (all-purpose) flour
250ml/8fl oz/1 cup milk
50g/2oz/½ cup grated mature (sharp)
   Cheddar cheese
4 eggs, separated
2 sun-dried tomatoes in oil, drained
   and chopped
15ml/1 tbsp chopped fresh chives
salt and ground black pepper

1 Place the ceps in a bowl, pour over enough warm water to cover and leave to soak for 15 minutes. Grease four individual earthenware soufflé dishes with a little butter. Sprinkle the grated Parmesan cheese into the soufflé dishes and rotate each dish to coat the sides with cheese. Preheat the oven to 190°C/375°F/Gas 5.

2 Melt the 40g/1½oz/3 tbsp of butter in a large pan, remove from the heat and stir in the flour. Cook over a low heat for 1 minute, stirring constantly. Remove the pan from the heat and gradually stir in the milk. Return to the heat and bring to the boil, stirring constantly, until the sauce has thickened.

COOK'S TIP
A variety of different dried mushrooms are available – any can be used instead of the ceps.

3 Remove the sauce from the heat, then stir in the grated Cheddar cheese and plenty of seasoning. Beat in the egg yolks, one at a time, then stir in the chopped sun-dried tomatoes and the chives. Drain the soaked mushrooms, then coarsely chop them and add them to the cheese sauce.

4 Whisk the egg whites until they stand in soft peaks. Mix one spoonful into the sauce then carefully fold in the remainder. Divide the mixture among the soufflé dishes and bake for 25 minutes, or until the soufflés are golden brown on top, well risen and just firm to the touch. Serve immediately – before they sink.

BRAISED VINE LEAVES

This popular eastern Mediterranean dish keeps moist when cooked slowly in a clay pot.

SERVES 4

12 fresh vine leaves
30ml/2 tbsp olive oil
1 small onion, chopped
30ml/2 tbsp pine nuts
1 garlic clove, crushed
115g/4oz cooked long grain rice
2 tomatoes, skinned, seeded and
    finely chopped
15ml/1 tbsp chopped fresh mint
1 lemon, sliced
150ml/¼ pint/⅔ cup dry white wine
200ml/7fl oz/scant 1 cup vegetable stock
salt and ground black pepper
lemon wedges, to serve

1 Soak the clay pot in cold water for 20 minutes, then drain. Blanch the vine leaves in a pan of boiling water for about 2 minutes or until they darken and soften. Rinse the leaves under cold running water and leave to drain.

2 Heat the oil in a frying pan, add the onion and fry for 5–6 minutes, stirring frequently, until softened. Add the pine nuts and crushed garlic and cook, stirring continuously until the onions and pine nuts are a golden brown colour.

3 Stir the onion mixture into the rice, with the tomatoes, mint and seasoning.

4 Place a spoonful of the rice mixture at the stalk end of each vine leaf. Fold the sides over the filling and roll up tightly.

5 Place the stuffed vine leaves close together, seam side down in the clay pot. Place the lemon slices on top. Pour over the wine and sufficient stock to just cover the lemon slices.

6 Cover with the lid and place in an unheated oven. Set the oven to 200°C/ 400°F/Gas 6 and cook for 30 minutes. Reduce to 160°C/325°F/Gas 3 and cook for a further 30 minutes. Serve hot or cold, with lemon wedges.

POTATO WEDGES with TOMATO and CHILLI SALSA

This is a healthier version of traditionally baked potato skins; the clay pot keeps the potato flesh wonderfully moist and fluffy.

SERVES 4

6 potatoes, about 115g/4oz each
45ml/3 tbsp olive oil
salt and ground black pepper

For the tomato and chilli salsa
4 juicy ripe tomatoes
1 sun-dried tomato in olive
   oil, drained
3 spring onions (scallions)
1–2 red or green chillies, halved
   and seeded
15ml/1 tbsp extra virgin
   olive oil
10ml/2 tsp lemon juice

COOK'S TIP
Varieties of floury potatoes that produce a fluffy texture when baked are best for these wedges. Good types to use include Maris Piper, Désirée, King Edward and Pentland Squire.

1 Soak the clay pot or a potato pot in cold water for 20 minutes, then drain. Scrub the potatoes and dry with kitchen paper. Cut each potato lengthwise into four wedges. Brush with a little of the oil and sprinkle with salt and pepper.

2 Place the potatoes in the clay pot and cover with the lid. Place in an unheated oven, set the temperature to 200°C/400°F/Gas 6 and cook for 55–60 minutes, or until the potatoes are tender.

3 Meanwhile, finely chop the tomatoes, sun-dried tomato, spring onions and chilli and mix together with the olive oil and lemon juice. Cover and leave to stand to allow the flavours to mingle.

4 Uncover the potatoes, brush with the remaining olive oil and bake, uncovered, for a further 15 minutes until slightly golden. Divide the potato wedges and salsa among four serving bowls and plates, and serve immediately.

SAFFRON MUSSELS with WHITE WINE and GARLIC

Mussels are easy to cook in a clay pot and they stay deliciously moist. The saffron adds a lovely pungent flavour as well as its characteristic yellow colour to the creamy sauce.

SERVES 4

few threads of saffron
1kg/2¼lb mussels in their shells
25g/1oz/2 tbsp butter
2 shallots, finely chopped
2 garlic cloves, finely chopped
200ml/7fl oz/scant 1 cup dry white wine
60ml/4 tbsp double (heavy) cream or
   crème fraîche
30ml/2 tbsp chopped fresh parsley
salt and ground black pepper
French bread, to serve

1 Soak a large clay pot in cold water for about 20 minutes, then drain. Put the saffron in a small bowl, add 15ml/1 tbsp boiling water and leave to soak.

2 Scrub the mussels, pull off the beards and discard any open mussels that don't close when tapped. Place all the closed mussels in the soaked clay pot.

3 Melt the butter in a frying pan, add the shallots and garlic and cook gently for 5 minutes, to soften. Stir in the wine and saffron water and bring to the boil. Pour the liquid over the mussels.

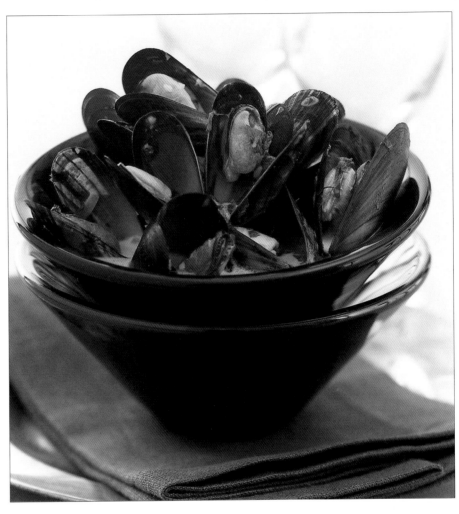

4 Cover the clay pot and place in an unheated oven. Set the oven to 220°C/425°F/Gas 7. Cook the mussels for 15 minutes, then remove the pot from the oven and, firmly holding the lid on, shake the pot. Return the pot to the oven and cook for another 10 minutes, or until the mussels have opened.

COOK'S TIP
Saffron is the stigma of a type of crocus. It is an expensive spice and is sold as thin, wiry threads. It has a mild aroma and adds a slightly pungent flavour to both sweet and savoury dishes, and also to buns, cakes and breads. However, the main characteristic of saffron is the distinctive yellow colour it imparts once diluted in a liquid.

5 Using a slotted spoon, transfer the mussels to four warmed serving bowls (discard any that have not opened). Mix the cream or crème fraîche and parsley into the cooking liquid and season to taste. Pour the cooking liquid over the mussels and serve immediately with French bread to soak up the sauce.

PRAWNS with BAKED GARLIC and ROASTED TOMATOES

Packed full of wonderful Mediterranean flavours, this simple, gutsy dish makes a marvellous first course for a dinner party.

SERVES 4

4 small garlic bulbs
60–75ml/4–5 tbsp olive oil
500g/1¼lb baby plum tomatoes on
   the vine
16 raw large prawns (jumbo shrimp), in
   their shells
a few sprigs of fresh thyme
salt and ground black pepper
lemon wedges and warm crusty bread,
   to serve

COOK'S TIPS
• If you can't find small garlic bulbs use
one large one and bake it in the oven for
about 50 minutes, or until the cloves are
soft and creamy.
• Spread a little of the baked garlic on the
bread and drizzle with olive oil.

1 Cut a small cross in the top of each bulb of garlic. Place the bulbs in a garlic baker, brush with half the olive oil and sprinkle with a little salt and ground black pepper.

2 Place the garlic baker in an unheated oven, set the temperature to 200°C/400°F/Gas 6 and bake the garlic for about 40 minutes. The garlic cloves should be soft and creamy – if not, bake for a further 10 minutes.

3 Place the tomatoes and prawns in a shallow earthenware baking dish. Drizzle over the remaining olive oil, sprinkle with thyme sprigs and season. Place the dish in the oven after the garlic has been cooking for 30 minutes; turn the prawns after 7 minutes.

4 Arrange the garlic, tomatoes and prawns on a warmed serving plate and serve with lemon wedges and plenty of crusty bread.

PORK RIBS with GINGER and CHILLI

Ginger, garlic and chilli are used to flavour the sweet-and-sour sauce that coats these ribs. Cook the pork ribs in a covered clay pot first to tenderize the meat, then uncover the dish so the ribs become deliciously sticky and brown.

SERVES 4

16–20 small meaty pork ribs, about
  900g/2lb total weight
1 onion, finely chopped
5cm/2in piece fresh root ginger, peeled
  and grated
2 garlic cloves, crushed
2.5–5ml/½–1 tsp chilli powder
60ml/4 tbsp soy sauce
45ml/3 tbsp tomato purée (paste)
45ml/3 tbsp clear honey
30ml/2 tbsp red wine vinegar
45ml/3 tbsp dry sherry
60ml/4 tbsp water
salt and ground black pepper

1 Soak the clay pot in cold water for 20 minutes, then drain. Place the ribs in the clay pot, arranging them evenly.

2 Mix together the onion, ginger, garlic, chilli powder, soy sauce, tomato purée, honey, wine vinegar, sherry and water.

3 Pour the sauce over the ribs and toss to coat them. Cover the clay pot and place in an unheated oven. Set the oven to 220°C/425°F/Gas 7. Cook for 1 hour.

4 Remove the lid, baste the ribs and season with salt and pepper. Cook uncovered for 15–20 minutes, basting the ribs two to three times during the cooking. Serve with steamed rice or baked potatoes.

COOK'S TIPS
• For a stronger flavour, place the ribs in a shallow dish, coat them evenly with the sauce and leave to marinate in a cool place for 1–2 hours before cooking in the clay pot.
• If you cannot get hold of fresh root ginger, ginger in sunflower oil (sold in small jars) is available from major supermarkets. It is in a paste form and can simply be added when the flavour of fresh root ginger is required. Use 10ml/ 2 tsp instead of 5cm/2in of fresh ginger.

HEARTY MAIN MEALS

Nothing quite matches the flavour of meat that has simmered in the oven for hours with tasty root vegetables and aromatic herbs to make sustaining stews such as Beef Hotpot with Herb Dumplings or Poussins and New Potato Pot-Roast. If you are feeling more adventurous, there's the Creole dish Chicken Gumbo with Okra, Ham, Tomatoes and Prawns, or the equally delicious Fragrant Lamb Curry with Cardamon-spiced Rice.

CLAY-POT BEEF with RED PEPPERS

Using a clay pot to cook lean meat keeps it moist and juicy. Here it is cooked with sweet peppers and onion in a rich red wine sauce.

SERVES 6

1.2kg/2½lb top rump (round) steak
   or silverside (pot roast) of beef,
   neatly tied
2 garlic cloves
30ml/2 tbsp sunflower oil
1 large onion, chopped
300ml/½ pint/1¼ cups beef stock
15ml/1 tbsp tomato purée (paste)
150ml/¼ pint/⅔ cup red wine
bouquet garni
4 sweet romano red (bell) peppers, halved
   lengthwise and seeded
15ml/1 tbsp butter, softened
15ml/1 tbsp plain (all-purpose) flour
salt and ground black pepper

1 Soak the clay pot in cold water for 20 minutes, then drain. Using a sharp knife, make about 20 small incisions in the beef. Cut the garlic cloves into thin slivers and insert into the cuts.

2 Season the beef with salt and pepper. Heat the sunflower oil in a large frying pan, add the beef and cook, stirring frequently with a wooden spoon until browned on all sides. Remove the beef from the pan and set aside.

3 Add the onion to the frying pan and fry gently for 5–8 minutes, stirring occasionally, until light golden. Transfer the onion to the clay pot.

4 Place the beef on top of the onion in the clay pot, then mix together the beef stock, tomato purée and wine and pour over the beef.

5 Add the bouquet garni to the pot, then cover the pot and place it in an unheated oven. Set the oven to 200°C/ 400°F/Gas 6 and cook for 1 hour. Uncover, baste the meat and add the pepper halves, arranging them around the meat. Cook uncovered for a further 45 minutes until the beef is tender, basting occasionally.

6 To serve, transfer the beef to a large warmed serving dish with the peppers and onion. Drain the juices from the clay pot into a pan and heat gently.

7 Blend together the butter and flour to make a smooth paste, then gradually add small pieces of the paste to the sauce, whisking until well blended. Bring the sauce to the boil and simmer gently for about 1 minute, whisking all the time, until the sauce is thickened slightly. Pour into a sauce boat and serve with the beef and vegetables.

VARIATIONS

Romano peppers are an elongated variety that are available in large supermarkets. If you can't find them, use ordinary bell-shaped peppers instead – the dish will be just as good. If you prefer, use green, orange or yellow peppers in place of red.

COOK'S TIPS

• The butter and flour paste used in step 7 to thicken the sauce is known as a beurre manié. The paste is always made from equal quantities of plain flour and softened butter. It is used for thickening casseroles, sauces and occasionally soups.
• A bouquet garni is a selection of aromatic herbs used to flavour soups, stocks or casseroles. The most widely used herbs include thyme, parsley, rosemary and bay leaves. Fresh herbs can be tied together with string or dried herbs can be wrapped in a small muslin (cheesecloth) square and secured with string. Ready-made bouquet garnis of dried herbs are sold in many supermarkets.

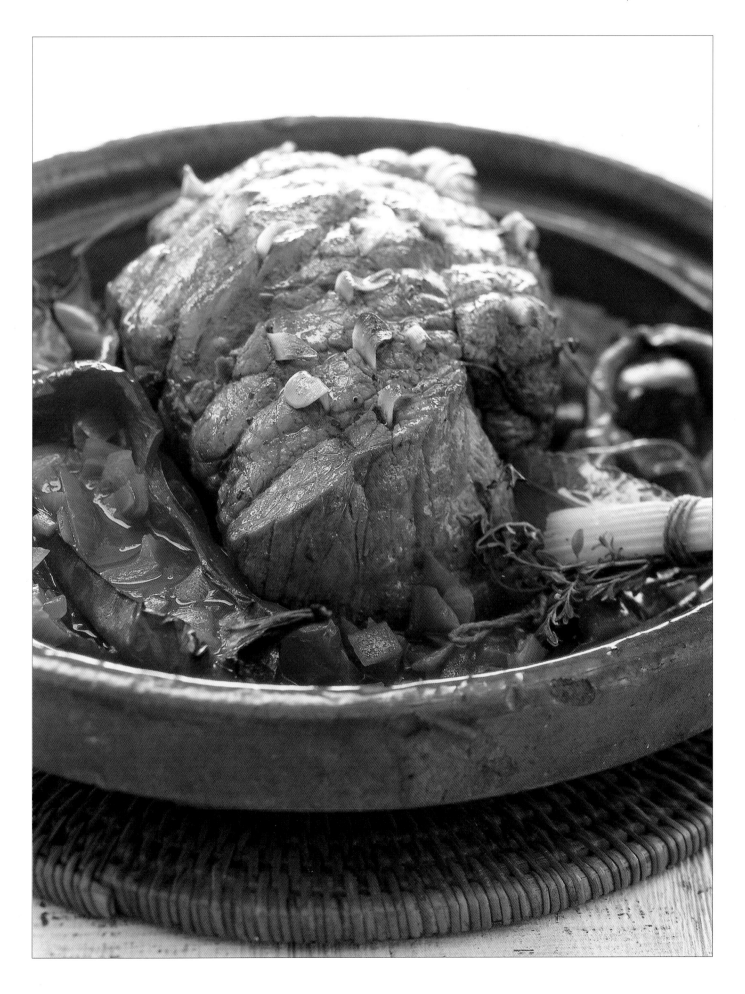

SLOW-BAKED BEEF with a POTATO CRUST

*This recipe makes the most of braising beef by marinating it in red wine and topping it
with a cheesy grated potato crust that bakes to a golden, crunchy consistency.*

SERVES 4

675g/1½lb stewing beef, diced
300ml/½ pint/1¼ cups red wine
3 juniper berries, crushed
pared strip of orange peel
30ml/2 tbsp olive oil
2 onions, cut into chunks
2 carrots, cut into chunks
1 garlic clove, crushed
225g/8oz/3 cups button
    (white) mushrooms
150ml/¼ pint/⅔ cup beef stock
30ml/2 tbsp cornflour (cornstarch)
salt and ground black pepper

For the crust
450g/1lb potatoes, grated
15ml/1 tbsp olive oil
30ml/2 tbsp creamed horseradish
50g/2oz/½ cup grated mature (sharp)
    Cheddar cheese
salt and ground black pepper

1 Place the diced beef in a non-metallic
bowl. Add the wine, juniper berries and
orange peel and season with pepper. Mix
the ingredients together, then cover and
leave to marinate for at least 4 hours or
overnight if possible.

COOK'S TIP
Use a large-holed, coarse grater on the
food processor for the potatoes. They
will hold their shape better while being
blanched than if you use a finer blade.

2 Preheat the oven to 160°C/325°F/
Gas 3. Drain the diced stewing beef,
reserving the marinade.

3 Heat the oil in a large flameproof
casserole and fry the meat in batches for
5 minutes to brown and seal. Add the
onions, carrots and garlic and cook for
5 minutes. Stir in the mushrooms, red
wine marinade and beef stock.

4 Mix the cornflour with water to make
a smooth paste and stir into the beef
mixture. Season, cover and cook in the
oven for 1½ hours.

5 Prepare the crust about 45 minutes
before the end of the cooking time for
the beef. Start by blanching the grated
potatoes in boiling water for 5 minutes.
Drain well and then squeeze out all the
extra liquid.

6 Stir in the olive oil, horseradish, grated
cheese and seasoning, then sprinkle the
mixture evenly over the surface of the
beef. Increase the oven temperature
to 200°C/400°F/Gas 6 and cook for a
further 30 minutes until the potato crust
is crisp and lightly browned.

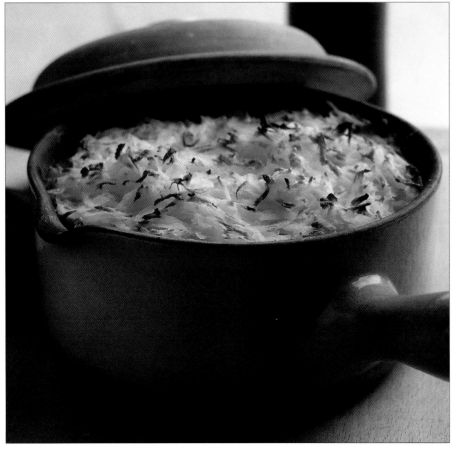

BEEF HOTPOT with HERB DUMPLINGS

Tender chunks of beef braised in beer, flavoured with shallots and mushrooms and finished with parsley- and thyme-flavoured dumplings.

SERVES 4

20g/¾oz/⅓ cup dried porcini mushrooms
60ml/4 tbsp warm water
40g/1½oz/3 tbsp butter
30ml/2 tbsp sunflower oil
115g/4oz/⅔ cup lardons or cubed pancetta
900g/2lb lean braising steak, cut
   into chunks
45ml/3 tbsp plain (all-purpose) flour
450ml/¾ pint/scant 2 cups beer
450ml/¾ pint/scant 2 cups beef stock
bouquet garni
8 shallots
175g/6oz/2 cups button (white) mushrooms
salt and ground black pepper
sprigs of thyme, to garnish

For the herb dumplings
115g/4oz/1 cup self-raising
   (self-rising) flour
50g/2oz/scant ½ cup shredded suet
2.5ml/½ tsp salt
2.5ml/½ tsp mustard powder
15ml/1 tbsp chopped fresh parsley
15ml/1 tbsp chopped fresh thyme

1 Soak a clay pot in cold water for 20 minutes, then drain. Place the porcini mushrooms in a bowl, add the warm water and leave to soak. In a frying pan, melt half the butter with half the oil, add the lardons or pancetta and quickly brown. Remove with a slotted spoon and transfer to the clay pot.

2 Add the beef to the frying pan and brown in batches, then, using a slotted spoon, transfer to the clay pot. Sprinkle the flour into the fat remaining in the frying pan and stir well.

3 Stir the beer and stock into the flour and bring to the boil, stirring constantly. Strain the mushroom soaking liquid and add to the frying pan along with the porcini. Season well. Pour the sauce over the meat in the clay pot, then add the bouquet garni. Cover the pot and place in an unheated oven. Set the oven to 200°C/400°F/Gas 6. Cook for 30 minutes, then reduce the oven temperature to 160°C/325°F/Gas 3 and cook for a further 1 hour.

4 Heat the remaining butter and oil in a frying pan and cook the shallots until golden. Remove and set aside. Add the button mushrooms and sauté for 2–3 minutes. Stir the shallots and mushrooms into the pot and cook for 30 minutes.

5 In a bowl, mix together the dumpling ingredients with sufficient cold water to bind to a soft, sticky dough. Divide into 12 small balls and place on top of the hotpot. Cover and cook for 25 minutes.

LAMB SHANKS with BEANS and HERBS

A hearty winter meal, the lamb shanks are slowly cooked in a clay pot until tender on a bed of tasty beans and vegetables.

SERVES 4

175g/6oz/1 cup dried cannellini beans,
　　soaked overnight in cold water
150ml/¼ pint/⅔ cup water
45ml/3 tbsp olive oil
4 large lamb shanks, about 225g/8oz each
1 large onion, chopped
450g/1lb carrots, cut into thick chunks
2 celery sticks, cut into thick chunks
450g/1lb tomatoes, quartered
250ml/8fl oz/1 cup vegetable stock
4 fresh rosemary sprigs
2 bay leaves
salt and ground black pepper

1 Soak a large clay pot in cold water for 20 minutes, then drain. Drain and rinse the cannellini beans and place in a large pan of unsalted boiling water and boil rapidly for 10 minutes, then drain.

2 Place the 150ml/¼ pint/⅔ cup water in the soaked clay pot and then add the drained cannellini beans.

3 Heat 30ml/2 tbsp of the olive oil in a large frying pan, add the lamb shanks and cook over a high heat, turning the lamb shanks occasionally until brown on all sides. Remove the lamb shanks with a slotted spoon and set aside.

4 Add the remaining oil to the pan, then add the onion and sauté for 5 minutes, until soft and translucent.

5 Add the carrots and celery to the pan and cook for 2–3 minutes. Stir in the quartered tomatoes and vegetable stock and mix well. Transfer the vegetable mixture to the clay pot and season well with salt and pepper, then add the fresh rosemary and bay leaves and stir again to combine.

6 Place the lamb shanks on top of the beans and vegetables. Cover the clay pot and place it in an unheated oven. Set the oven to 220°C/425°F/Gas 7 and cook for about 30 minutes, or until the liquid is bubbling.

7 Reduce the oven temperature to 160°C/325°F/Gas 3 and cook for about 1½ hours, or until the meat is tender. Check the seasoning and serve on warmed plates, placing each lamb shank on a bed of beans and vegetables.

COOK'S TIP

Lamb shanks are small joints cut from the lower end of the leg. One shank is an ideal-sized portion for one. Until recently you would have had to order them from the butcher, but they are now becoming increasingly available from larger supermarkets. To obtain a tender result, shanks should be cooked for a long time at a low heat.

VARIATIONS

• Dried butter (lima) beans or the smaller haricot (navy) beans can be used in place of the cannellini beans.
• If you prefer, two 400g/14oz cans cannellini beans can be used in this dish – simply place the drained beans in the soaked clay pot with the water and continue from step 3.
• A variety of other root vegetables would work well in this recipe – try chopped swede (rutabaga), sweet potatoes, butternut squash, parsnips or celeriac instead of the carrots. In spring, a mixture of baby turnips and baby carrots would also be good.

FRAGRANT LAMB CURRY with CARDAMOM-SPICED RICE

Wonderfully aromatic, this Indian-style lamb biriani, with the meat and rice cooked together, is a delicious meal in itself.

SERVES 4

1 large onion, quartered
2 garlic cloves
1 small green chilli, halved and seeded
5cm/2in piece fresh root ginger
15ml/1 tbsp ghee
15ml/1 tbsp vegetable oil
675 g/1½lb boned shoulder or leg of lamb,
   cut into chunks
15ml/1 tbsp ground coriander
10ml/2 tsp ground cumin
1 cinnamon stick, broken into 3 pieces
150ml/¼ pint/⅔ cup thick natural
   (plain) yogurt
150ml/¼ pint/⅔ cup water
75g/3oz/⅓ cup ready-to-eat dried apricots,
   cut into chunks
salt and ground black pepper

For the rice
250g/9oz/1¼ cups basmati rice
6 cardamom pods, split open
25g/1oz/2 tbsp butter, cut into small pieces
45ml/3 tbsp toasted cashew nuts or flaked
   (sliced) almonds

For the garnish
1 onion, sliced and fried until golden
a few sprigs of fresh coriander (cilantro)

1 Soak a large clay pot or chicken brick in cold water for 20 minutes, then drain. Place the onion, garlic, chilli and ginger in a food processor or blender and process with 15ml/1 tbsp water, to a smooth paste.

COOK'S TIP
Serve a cooling yogurt raita and a fresh fruit chutney or relish as an accompaniment.

2 Heat the ghee and vegetable oil in a heavy frying pan. Fry the lamb chunks in batches over a high heat until golden brown. Remove from the pan using a slotted spoon and set aside.

3 Add the onion paste to the remaining oil left in the frying pan, stir in the ground coriander and cumin, add the cinnamon stick pieces and fry for 1–2 minutes, stirring constantly with a wooden spoon.

4 Return the meat to the frying pan, then gradually add the yogurt, a spoonful at a time, stirring well between each addition with a wooden spoon. Season the meat well with plenty of salt and pepper and stir in the water.

5 Transfer the contents of the frying pan to the prepared clay pot, cover with the lid and place in an unheated oven. Set the oven to 180°C/350°F/Gas 4 and cook for 45 minutes.

6 Meanwhile prepare the basmati rice. Place it in a bowl, cover with cold water and leave to soak for 20 minutes. Drain the rice and place it in a large pan of boiling salted water, bring back to the boil and cook for 10 minutes. Drain and stir in the split cardamom pods.

7 Remove the clay pot from the oven and stir in the chopped ready-to-eat apricots. Pile the cooked rice on top of the lamb and dot with the butter. Drizzle over 60ml/4 tbsp water, then sprinkle the cashew nuts or flaked almonds on top. Cover the pot, reduce the oven temperature to 150°C/300°F/Gas 2 and cook the meat and rice for 30 minutes.

8 Remove the lid from the pot and fluff up the rice with a fork. Spoon into warmed individual bowls, then sprinkle over the fried onion slices and garnish with the sprigs of fresh coriander.

ITALIAN LAMB MEATBALLS with CHILLI TOMATO SAUCE

Serve these piquant Italian-style meatballs with pasta and a leafy salad. Sprinkle with a little grated Parmesan cheese for that extra Italian touch.

SERVES 4

450g/1lb lean minced (ground) lamb
1 large onion, grated
1 garlic clove, crushed
50g/2oz/1 cup fresh white breadcrumbs
15ml/1 tbsp chopped fresh parsley
1 small egg, lightly beaten
30ml/2 tbsp olive oil
salt and ground black pepper
60ml/4 tbsp finely grated Parmesan cheese
   and rocket (arugula) leaves, to serve

For the sauce
1 onion, finely chopped
400g/14oz can chopped tomatoes
200ml/7fl oz/scant 1 cup passata (bottled
   strained tomatoes)
5ml/1 tsp granulated sugar
2 green chillies, seeded and finely chopped
30ml/2 tbsp chopped fresh oregano
salt and ground black pepper

1 Soak a small clay pot in cold water for 15 minutes, then drain. Place the minced lamb, onion, garlic, breadcrumbs, parsley and seasoning in a bowl and mix well. Add the beaten egg and mix to bind the meatball mixture together.

2 Shape the mixture into 20 small even-size balls. Heat the olive oil in a frying pan, add the meatballs and cook over a high heat, stirring occasionally, until they are browned all over.

VARIATIONS
Minced (ground) beef or sausage meat (bulk sausage) can be used in place of the minced lamb in this dish.

3 Meanwhile, to make the sauce, mix together the chopped onion, tomatoes, passata, sugar, seeded and chopped chillies and oregano. Season well and pour the sauce into the clay pot.

4 Place the meatballs in the sauce, then cover and place in an unheated oven. Set the oven to 200°C/400°F/Gas 6 and cook for 1 hour, stirring after 30 minutes. Serve with Parmesan cheese and rocket.

POTATO and SAUSAGE CASSEROLE

You will find numerous variations of this traditional supper dish throughout Ireland, but the basic ingredients are the same wherever you go – potatoes, sausages and bacon.

2 Heat the oil in a frying pan, then add the bacon and fry for 2 minutes, stirring. Add the onions and fry for 5–6 minutes until golden. Add the garlic and fry for 1 minute, then remove the mixture from the pan and set aside.

3 Fry the sausages in the same pan for 5–6 minutes until golden brown.

SERVES 4

15ml/1 tbsp vegetable oil
4 bacon rashers (strips), cut into
   2.5cm/1in pieces
2 large onions, chopped
2 garlic cloves, crushed
8 large pork sausages
4 large baking potatoes, peeled and
   thinly sliced
1.5ml/¼ tsp fresh sage
300ml/½ pint/1¼ cups vegetable stock
salt and ground black pepper
crusty bread, to serve

1 Preheat the oven to 180°C/350°F/ Gas 4. Lightly grease a large, shallow earthenware baking dish and set aside.

4 Arrange the potatoes in the base of the prepared dish. Spoon the bacon and onion mixture on top. Season with the salt and pepper and sprinkle with the fresh sage. Pour on the stock and top with the sausages. Cover and bake for about 1 hour, or until the potatoes and sausages are tender. Serve hot with crusty bread.

PORK TENDERLOIN with SPINACH and PUY LENTILS

Lean pork tenderloin, wrapped in spinach and cooked in a clay pot on a bed of tiny French green lentils, flavoured with coconut.

SERVES 4

500–675g/1¼–1½lb pork tenderloin
15ml/1 tbsp sunflower oil
15g/½oz/1 tbsp butter
8–12 large spinach leaves
1 onion, chopped
1 garlic clove, finely chopped
2.5cm/1in piece fresh root ginger,
   finely grated
1 red chilli, finely chopped (optional)
250g/9oz/generous 1 cup Puy lentils
750ml/1¼ pints/3 cups chicken or
   vegetable stock
200ml/7fl oz/scant 1 cup coconut cream
salt and ground black pepper

3 Meanwhile, add the spinach leaves to a large pan of boiling water and cook for 1 minute, or until just wilted. Drain immediately in a colander and refresh under cold running water. Drain well.

6 Add the lentils to the onion mixture in the frying pan and then stir in the chicken or vegetable stock. Bring to the boil, then boil rapidly for 10 minutes. Remove the pan from the heat and stir in the coconut cream until well blended. Transfer the onion and lentil mixture to the clay pot and arrange the pork tenderloins on top.

7 Cover the clay pot and place it in an unheated oven. Set the oven to 190°C/375°F/Gas 5 and cook for 45 minutes, or until the lentils and pork are cooked.

1 Soak a small clay pot in cold water for about 15 minutes, then drain. Cut the pork tenderloin widthwise into two equal pieces. Season the pork well with salt and ground black pepper.

4 Lay the spinach leaves on the work surface, overlapping them slightly to form a rectangle. Place the pork on top and wrap the leaves around the pork to enclose it completely.

8 To serve, remove the spinach-wrapped pork tenderloins from the clay pot using a slotted spoon or tongs and cut the pork into thick slices. Stir the lentils and spoon them, with some of the cooking juices, on to warmed, individual plates and top each portion with a few of the pork slices.

VARIATIONS

• Wrap the pork in slices of prosciutto, instead of the spinach leaves, and tie in place with string or secure with wooden cocktail sticks (toothpicks).
• Use 4 large chicken or duck breast portions in place of the pork tenderloin. Check the chicken or duck after about 30 minutes cooking time. Cut the breast portions into thick, diagonal slices to serve. The chicken would also be good wrapped with prosciutto.

2 Heat the sunflower oil and butter in a heavy frying pan, add the pork tenderloin and cook over a high heat until browned on all sides. Remove the meat from the pan using a fish slice (spatula) and set aside.

5 Add the onion to the oil in the frying pan and cook for about 5 minutes, stirring occasionally, until softened. Add the chopped garlic, grated ginger and finely chopped chilli, if using, and fry for a further 1 minute.

STOVED CHICKEN

"Stovies" were originally potatoes slowly cooked on the stove with onions and dripping or butter until falling to pieces. This version includes a delicious layer of bacon and chicken.

2 Heat the butter and oil in a large, heavy frying pan, add the chopped bacon and chicken pieces and cook, turning occasionally, until brown on all sides. Using a slotted spoon, transfer the chicken and bacon to the earthenware dish. Reserve the fat in the pan.

3 Sprinkle the remaining chopped thyme over the chicken, season with salt and pepper, then cover with the remaining onion slices, followed by a neat, overlapping layer of the remaining potato slices. Season the top layer of potatoes with more salt and ground black pepper.

SERVES 4

1kg/2¼lb baking potatoes, cut into
  5mm/¼in slices
butter, for greasing
2 large onions, thinly sliced
15ml/1 tbsp chopped fresh thyme
25g/1oz/2 tbsp butter
15ml/1 tbsp vegetable oil
2 large bacon rashers (strips), chopped
4 large chicken portions, halved
600ml/1 pint/2½ cups chicken stock
1 bay leaf
salt and ground black pepper

COOK'S TIP

Instead of chicken portions, choose eight chicken thighs or chicken drumsticks.

1 Preheat the oven to 150°C/300°F/ Gas 2. Arrange a thick layer of half the potato slices in a large lightly greased, earthenware baking dish, then cover with half the onions. Sprinkle with half of the thyme, and season with salt and pepper to taste.

4 Pour the chicken stock into the casserole, add the bay leaf and brush the potatoes with the reserved fat from the frying pan. Cover tightly with foil and bake for about 2 hours, or until the chicken is cooked and tender.

5 Preheat the grill (broiler) to medium-hot, then remove the foil from the earthenware dish and place the dish under the grill. Cook until the slices of potato are beginning to turn golden brown and crisp. Remove the bay leaf and serve immediately.

CORN-FED CHICKEN with WINTER VEGETABLES

Chicken cooked in a clay pot remains beautifully moist and tender. Flavoured with lemon, parsley and tarragon, serve this as an alternative to a traditional Sunday roast.

SERVES 4

3 large carrots, cut into batons
1 celery heart, thickly sliced
2 red onions, quartered
a few sprigs of fresh thyme
1.6kg/3½lb corn-fed chicken
40g/1½oz/3 tbsp butter, softened
15ml/1 tbsp chopped fresh parsley
15ml/1 tbsp chopped fresh tarragon
1 small lemon, halved
300ml/½ pint/1¼ cups dry white wine or
    chicken stock
salt and ground black pepper

COOK'S TIP
Cook some potatoes in the oven at the same time to accompany the pot roast – baked potatoes or roast potatoes both go well with this main course. Or, if you prefer, serve the pot-roast with creamy mashed potatoes.

1 Soak a chicken brick or large clay pot in cold water for 20 minutes, then drain. Place the carrots, celery, red onions and thyme in the pot.

2 Wash the chicken and dry thoroughly. Mix together the butter, parsley and tarragon. Ease up the breast skin of the chicken and spread the butter under it, taking care not to puncture the skin. Place the lemon halves inside the chicken.

3 Rub the chicken with seasoning and nestle on top of the vegetables. Add the wine or chicken stock and cover. Place the chicken brick or pot in an unheated oven. Set the oven temperature to 200°C/400°F/Gas 6 and cook for about 1¾ hours, or until the chicken is cooked.

4 Remove the lid from the brick or pot and cook for a further 10 minutes, or until the chicken is golden brown.

CHICKEN GUMBO with OKRA, HAM, TOMATOES and PRAWNS

This classic Creole dish is really a very hearty soup, but is usually served over rice as a delicious and filling main course, like a stew.

SERVES 4

30ml/2 tbsp olive oil
1 onion, chopped
225g/8oz skinless, boneless chicken
    breast portions, cut into
    small chunks
25g/1oz/¼ cup plain (all-purpose) flour
5ml/1 tsp paprika
30ml/2 tbsp tomato purée (paste)
600ml/1 pint/2½ cups well-flavoured
    chicken stock
400g/14oz can chopped tomatoes
    with herbs
a few drops of Tabasco
175g/6oz okra
1 red, orange or yellow (bell) pepper,
    seeded and chopped
2 celery sticks, sliced
225g/8oz/1⅓ cups diced lean
    cooked ham
225g/8oz large prawns (shrimp), peeled,
    deveined and heads removed, but with
    tails intact
salt and ground black pepper
boiled rice, to serve

1 Soak a large clay pot or chicken brick in cold water for 20 minutes, then drain. Heat the oil in a large frying pan, add the chopped onion and cook over a medium heat for about 5 minutes, stirring occasionally, until softened and lightly golden.

2 Add the chicken chunks to the pan and sauté for 1–2 minutes, to seal. Stir in the flour, paprika and tomato purée and cook, stirring constantly, for 1–2 minutes.

3 Gradually add the stock, stirring constantly, then bring the sauce to the boil, stirring. Add the chopped tomatoes, then remove the pan from the heat. Add a few drops of Tabasco and season with salt and pepper.

4 Cut the okra pods in half if they are large, then add them to the clay pot or chicken brick with the chopped red, orange or yellow pepper and the sliced celery. Add the chicken and tomato mixture and stir well to mix.

5 Cover the clay pot or chicken brick and place it in an unheated oven. Set the oven to 200°C/400°F/Gas 6 and cook for 30 minutes.

6 Remove the clay pot or chicken brick from the oven, then add the diced ham and the prawns and stir well to combine. Cover the pot or brick and return it to the oven for about 10 minutes, or until the ham is heated through and the prawns are just cooked. To serve, spoon some freshly boiled rice into four warmed, individual serving plates or bowls and ladle over the gumbo.

VARIATIONS
Replace the cooked ham with crab meat or cooked and shelled mussels or, for a special occasion, replace the peeled prawns with crayfish and replace the ham with cooked and shelled oysters.

COOK'S TIPS
• Okra is a favourite ingredient in the southern states of the USA and in African and Caribbean cooking. When buying, look for firm, bright green pods that are less than 10cm/4in long. Larger pods may be slightly tough and fibrous. When cooked, okra produces a rather viscous substance that thickens the liquid in which it is cooked – an essential part of many traditional okra recipes.
• If you don't have a bottle of Tabasco sauce to hand, add about 2.5ml/½ tsp chilli powder, or a finely chopped fresh or dried chilli. Remove the seeds from the chilli if you would prefer the gumbo to be only medium-hot.

POUSSINS and NEW POTATO POT-ROAST

Pot roasts are traditionally associated with the colder months, but this delicious version is a simple summer dish that makes the most of new season potatoes.

SERVES 4

2 poussins, about 500g/1¼lb each
25g/1oz/2 tbsp butter
15ml/1 tbsp clear honey
500g/1¼lb small new potatoes
1 red onion, halved lengthwise and cut
   into thin wedges
4–5 small rosemary sprigs
2 bay leaves
1 lemon, cut into wedges
450ml/¾ pint/scant 2 cups hot
   chicken stock
salt and ground black pepper

1 Soak a clay chicken brick in cold water for 20 minutes, then drain. Cut the poussins in half, along the breast bone.

2 Melt the butter, mix it together with the honey and brush over the poussins. Season with salt and pepper.

3 Place the small new potatoes and onion wedges in the base of the chicken brick. Tuck the rosemary sprigs, bay leaves and lemon wedges in among the vegetables. Pour over the hot chicken stock (see Cook's Tip).

4 Place the halved poussins on top of the vegetables. Cover the chicken brick and place it in an unheated oven. Set the oven to 200°C/400°F/Gas 6 and cook for 55–60 minutes, or until the poussin juices run clear and the vegetables are tender. Uncover the chicken brick for the last 10 minutes of cooking to add more colour to the poussins, if necessary.

COOK'S TIPS
• Make sure the stock is hot, but not boiling when it is added to the chicken brick otherwise the chicken brick may crack.
• A poussin is a baby chicken – usually around 4–6 weeks old. Poussins can be cooked by grilling (broiling), roasting or pot-roasting, but are especially tender and moist cooked in a chicken brick.

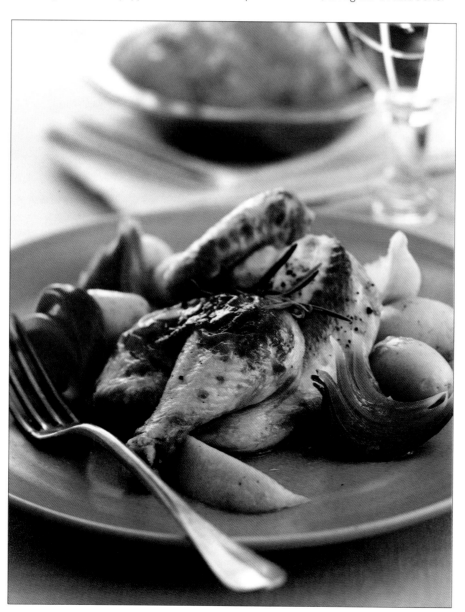

GUINEA FOWL with BEANS and CURLY KALE

Cooking lean poultry such as guinea fowl, chicken or turkey in a clay pot or chicken brick gives a delicious, moist result. Here the guinea fowl is cooked atop a colourful bed of herb-flavoured beans and vegetables.

2 Remove the shallots, garlic and celery with a slotted spoon and place in the chicken brick. Stir in the tomatoes and beans. Tuck in the thyme and bay leaves.

3 Put the guinea fowl in the frying pan and brown on all sides, then pour in the wine and stock and bring to the boil. Lift the bird out of the pan, place it on top of the vegetables in the chicken brick and then pour the liquid over the top. Cover and place in an unheated oven and set to 200°C/400°F/Gas 6. Cook for 1 hour.

4 Add the curly kale to the chicken brick, nestling it among the beans. Cover and cook for 10–15 minutes, or until the guinea fowl is tender. Season the bean mixture and serve.

COOK'S TIP

Guinea fowl and quail were both originally classified as game birds but nowadays farmed varieties are sold, making them available in the stores all year round.

VARIATION

Use chard, spring greens (collards) or Savoy cabbage in place of curly kale.

SERVES 4

1.3kg/3lb guinea fowl
45ml/3 tbsp olive oil
4 shallots, chopped
1 garlic clove, crushed
3 celery sticks, sliced
400g/14oz can chopped tomatoes
2 × 400g/14oz cans mixed
    beans, drained
5 fresh thyme sprigs
2 bay leaves
150ml/¼ pint/⅔ cup dry white wine
300ml/½ pint/1¼ cups well-flavoured
    chicken stock
175g/6oz curly kale
salt and ground black pepper

1 Soak a clay chicken brick in cold water for 20 minutes, then drain. Rub the guinea fowl with 15ml/1 tbsp of the olive oil and season. Place the remaining oil in a frying pan, add the shallots, garlic and celery and sauté for 4–5 minutes.

FISH AND SHELLFISH DISHES

Moist and succulent, fish tastes great when cooked in the oven, especially when baked in clay. Specially designed clay pots will hold a whole fish with ease, so you can treat yourself to Baked Sea Bass with Lemon Grass and Red Onions, or Monkfish with Rocket Pesto, Peppers and Onions. Also on the menu are delicious dishes such as Seafood Pie with Rösti Topping, a delectable potato and fish bake, and a very special Goan Fish Casserole.

GOAN FISH CASSEROLE

The cooking of Goa is a mixture of Portuguese and Indian; the addition of tamarind gives a slightly sour note to the spicy coconut sauce.

SERVES 4

7.5ml/1½ tsp ground turmeric
5ml/1 tsp salt
450g/1lb monkfish fillet, cut into
    eight pieces
15ml/1 tbsp lemon juice
5ml/1 tsp cumin seeds
5ml/1 tsp coriander seeds
5ml/1 tsp black peppercorns
1 garlic clove, chopped
5cm/2in piece fresh root ginger,
    finely chopped
25g/1oz tamarind paste
150ml/¼ pint/⅔ cup hot water
30ml/2 tbsp vegetable oil
2 onions, halved and sliced lengthways
400ml/14fl oz/1⅔ cups coconut milk
4 mild green chillies, seeded and cut into
    thin strips
16 large raw prawns (shrimp), peeled
30ml/2 tbsp chopped fresh coriander
    (cilantro) leaves, to garnish

1 Mix together the ground turmeric and salt in a small bowl. Place the monkfish in a shallow dish and sprinkle over the lemon juice, then rub the turmeric and salt mixture over the fish fillets to coat them completely. Cover and chill until ready to cook.

COOK'S TIP
Tamarind, which is also known as Indian date, is a popular spice throughout India, South-east Asia and the Caribbean. It has little smell, but the distinctive sour, yet fruity taste makes up for this. It is often used in curries and spicy dishes and is available from Indian and South-east Asian stores and some large supermarkets.

2 Put the cumin seeds, coriander seeds and black peppercorns in a blender or small food processor and blend to a powder. Add the garlic and ginger and process for a few seconds more.

3 Preheat the oven to 200°C/400°F/ Gas 6. Mix the tamarind paste with the hot water and set aside.

4 Heat the oil in a frying pan, add the onions and cook for 5–6 minutes, until softened and golden. Transfer the onions to a shallow earthenware dish.

VARIATION
You may use any firm white fish fillets such as cod, halibut or hake instead of the monkfish in this casserole.

5 Add the fish fillets to the oil remaining in the frying pan, and fry briefly over a high heat, turning them to seal on all sides. Remove the fish from the pan and place on top of the onions.

6 Add the ground spice mixture to the frying pan and cook over a medium heat, stirring constantly, for 1–2 minutes. Stir in the tamarind liquid, coconut milk and chilli strips and bring to the boil. Pour the sauce into the earthenware dish to coat the fish completely.

7 Cover the earthenware dish and cook the fish casserole in the oven for about 10 minutes. Add the prawns, pushing them into the liquid, then cover the dish again and return it to the oven for 5 minutes, or until the prawns turn pink. Do not overcook them or they will toughen. Check the seasoning, sprinkle with coriander leaves and serve.

BAKED SARDINES with CAPER and TOMATO STUFFING

Sardines are often a popular choice for cooking on the barbecue but you can enjoy these delicious Mediterranean-style baked sardines all year round.

SERVES 4

16 fresh sardines, cleaned
8–12 cherry tomatoes, on the vine, sliced
45ml/3 tbsp capers, chopped
½ small red onion, very finely chopped
60ml/4 tbsp olive oil
grated rind and juice 1 lemon
45ml/3 tbsp chopped fresh parsley
15ml/1 tbsp chopped fresh basil
basil sprigs and lemon wedges,
    to garnish
crusty bread, to serve

COOK'S TIP

Removing the bones before cooking, as in step 1 of this recipe, makes the sardines easier to eat.

1 Remove the backbone from the sardines by placing slit side down on a chopping board. Using your fingers, push firmly along the length of the backbone to loosen it from the flesh. Turn the sardine over and pull out the bone; cut the ends with a sharp knife to release it. Repeat with the remaining sardines.

2 Place the tomato slices inside each sardine; they may stick out slightly, depending on the size of the fish. Mix the capers and red onion together and place on top of the tomatoes.

3 Preheat the oven to 200°C/400°F/ Gas 6. Lay the sardines in a single layer in a large earthenware dish.

4 Mix together the olive oil, lemon rind and juice, parsley and basil and drizzle over the sardines. Bake the sardines for about 10 minutes, or until the fish flesh flakes easily. Garnish with basil and lemon wedges and serve with plenty of crusty bread to mop up the sauce.

SALMON BAKED with POTATOES and THYME

This is clay-pot cooking at its most sophisticated – a mouthwatering combination of potatoes and onions braised in thyme-flavoured stock and topped with perfectly tender pepper-crusted salmon fillets.

SERVES 4

675g/1½lb waxy potatoes, thinly sliced
1 onion, thinly sliced
10ml/2 tsp fresh thyme leaves
450ml/¾ pint/scant 2 cups vegetable or
    fish stock
40g/1½oz/3 tbsp butter,
    finely diced
4 skinless salmon fillets, about
    150g/5oz each
30ml/2 tbsp olive oil
15ml/1 tbsp black peppercorns,
    roughly crushed
salt and ground black pepper
fresh thyme, to garnish
mangetouts (snow peas) or sugar snap
    peas, to serve

1 Soak a fish clay pot in cold water for 20 minutes, then drain.

2 Layer the potato and onion slices in the clay pot, seasoning each layer and sprinkling with thyme. Pour over the stock, dot with butter, cover and place in an unheated oven.

3 Set the oven to 190°C/375°F/Gas 5. Bake the potatoes for 40 minutes then remove the lid and bake for a further 20 minutes, or until they are almost cooked.

4 Meanwhile brush the salmon fillets with olive oil and coat with crushed black peppercorns, pressing them in, if necessary, with the back of a spoon. Place the salmon on top of the potatoes, cover and cook for 15 minutes, or until the salmon is opaque, removing the lid for the last 5 minutes. Serve garnished with fresh thyme sprigs and with mangetouts or sugar snap peas to accompany.

MONKFISH with ROCKET PESTO, PEPPERS and ONIONS

Colourful Mediterranean vegetables complement richly flavoured monkfish layered with pesto sauce in this impressive-looking clay pot dish.

SERVES 4

900g/2lb monkfish tail
50g/2oz rocket (arugula)
30ml/2 tbsp pine nuts
1 garlic clove, chopped
25g/1oz/⅓ cup freshly grated
   Parmesan cheese
90ml/6 tbsp olive oil
45ml/3 tbsp lemon juice
2 red (bell) peppers, halved
2 yellow (bell) peppers, halved
1 red onion, cut into wedges
2 courgettes (zucchini), cut into
   2.5cm/1in slices
4 fresh rosemary sprigs
salt and ground black pepper

1 Remove any skin or membrane from the monkfish. Using a large, sharp knife cut along one side of the central bone, as close to the bone as possible and then remove the fish fillet. Repeat on the other side. Set aside.

2 Soak a fish clay pot in cold water for 20 minutes, then drain and set aside.

VARIATIONS
• Salmon tail fillets, or thick fillets of cod or haddock could be used in place of the monkfish. Remove the skin from the fish and run your hand along the other side to check for any hidden bones and, if necessary, remove these with tweezers.
• Rocket makes an interestingly peppery pesto, but other leafy herbs can be used to make this sauce. basil is the classic choice, but flat leaf parsley is also good.

3 Place the rocket, pine nuts, chopped garlic, freshly grated Parmesan cheese, 45ml/3 tbsp of the olive oil and 15ml/1 tbsp of the lemon juice in a food processor or blender and process to form a smooth paste.

4 Lay one fish fillet out flat, cut-side up and spread with the pesto. Place the remaining fillet on top, cut-side down, on top of the layer of pesto. Tie the fish with string at regular intervals to seal together. Sprinkle with plenty of salt and pepper to season and set aside.

5 Cut each pepper half into three lengthwise. Remove the core and seeds.

6 Place the pieces of pepper in the clay pot with the onion wedges and slices of courgette. In a small bowl, mix together 15ml/1 tbsp of the olive oil and the remaining lemon juice and sprinkle over the vegetables. Mix well and season with salt and plenty of black pepper.

7 Tuck the fresh rosemary sprigs in among the vegetables. Cover the clay pot and place in an unheated oven. Set the temperature to 220°C/425°F/Gas 7 and cook the vegetables for 20 minutes.

8 Remove the clay pot from the oven, place the monkfish parcel in the centre of the vegetables and brush it with 15ml/1 tbsp of the olive oil. Sprinkle the remaining oil over the vegetables. Cover the pot again, then return the pot to the oven and cook for 20–25 minutes more, or until the monkfish is cooked through and turns opaque.

9 To serve, cut the fish into thick slices, removing the string, if you prefer, and serve with the cooked vegetables.

BAKED SEA BASS with LEMON GRASS and RED ONIONS

Moist, tender sea bass is flavoured with a combination of traditional Thai ingredients in this simple but mouthwatering clay-pot dish.

SERVES 2–3

1 sea bass, about 675g/1½lb, cleaned
   and scaled
30ml/2 tbsp olive oil
2 lemon grass stalks, finely sliced
1 red onion, finely shredded
1 chilli, seeded and finely chopped
5cm/2in piece fresh root ginger,
   finely shredded
45ml/3 tbsp chopped fresh
   coriander (cilantro)
rind and juice of 2 limes
30ml/2 tbsp light soy sauce
salt and ground black pepper

COOK'S TIP
This recipe will taste delicious using a variety of fish, such as red or grey mullet, red snapper, salmon or tilapia. Depending on the weight of the fish you may need to use two smaller fish rather than one whole one.

1 Soak a fish clay pot in cold water for 20 minutes, then drain. Make four to five diagonal slashes on both sides of the fish. Repeat the slashes on one side in the opposite direction to give an attractive cross-hatched effect. Rub the sea bass inside and out with salt, pepper and 15ml/1 tbsp of the olive oil.

2 Mix together the Thai ingredients – the lemon grass, red onion, chilli, ginger, coriander and lime rind.

3 Place a little of the lemon grass and red onion mixture in the base of the clay pot, then lay the fish on top. Sprinkle the remaining mixture over the fish, then sprinkle over the lime juice, soy sauce and the remaining olive oil. Cover and place in an unheated oven.

4 Set the oven to 220°C/425°F/Gas 7 and cook the fish for 30–40 minutes, or until the flesh flakes easily when tested with a knife. Serve immediately.

SWORDFISH STEAKS with MANGO and AVOCADO SALSA

Meaty swordfish steaks, marinated in a tangy mix of lime juice, coriander and chilli, served with a vibrant fruity salsa.

SERVES 4

4 swordfish steaks, about 150g/5oz each
lime wedges and shredded spring onions
    (scallions), to garnish

For the marinade
rind and juice of 2 limes
2 garlic cloves, crushed
1 red chilli, seeded and finely chopped
30ml/2 tbsp olive oil
30ml/2 tbsp chopped fresh
    coriander (cilantro)
salt and ground black pepper

For the salsa
1 mango
4 spring onions (scallions), thinly sliced
1 red chilli, seeded and finely chopped
30ml/2 tbsp chopped fresh dill or
    coriander (cilantro)
30ml/2 tbsp lime juice
30ml/2 tbsp olive oil
1 ripe avocado

1 Place the swordfish steaks in a shallow non-metallic dish. Mix together the marinade ingredients and pour over the swordfish. Cover and leave to marinate in the refrigerator for 2 hours, or longer if time allows.

2 Soak a fish clay pot in cold water for 20 minutes, then drain. To prepare the salsa, peel the mango and slice the flesh off the stone (pit). Cut the flesh into rough dice. Add the spring onions, chilli, dill or coriander, lime juice and olive oil. Toss the ingredients together, cover and set aside to allow the flavours to blend.

3 Place the swordfish steaks in the clay pot and pour over the marinade. Cover and place in an unheated oven. Set the oven to 220°C/425°F/Gas 7 and bake for 15–20 minutes, or until the fish is cooked. The time will vary depending on the thickness of the steaks.

4 To complete the salsa, using a sharp knife, cut the avocado in half, remove the stone (pit), then roughly dice the flesh. Stir it into the prepared salsa ingredients and mix well. Serve the swordfish steaks with a mound of salsa, garnished with lime wedges and shredded spring onions.

SEAFOOD PIE with RÖSTI TOPPING

In this variation of a classic fish pie, a mixture of white fish and shellfish are combined with a creamy herb-flavoured sauce and finished with a grated potato topping.

SERVES 4

750g/1lb 10oz potatoes, unpeeled
    and scrubbed
50g/2oz/¼ cup butter, melted
350g/12oz cod or haddock fillets, skinned
    and cut into bitesize pieces
115g/4oz cooked, peeled prawns (shrimp)
115g/4oz cooked, shelled mussels
8–12 shelled queen scallops
50g/2oz/¼ cup butter
1 onion, finely chopped
50g/2oz/½ cup plain (all-purpose) flour
200ml/7fl oz/scant 1 cup dry white wine
300ml/½ pint/1¼ cups fish or
    vegetable stock
105ml/7 tbsp double (heavy) cream
30ml/2 tbsp chopped fresh dill, plus extra
    sprigs to garnish
15ml/1 tbsp chopped fresh parsley
60ml/4 tbsp freshly grated
    Parmesan cheese
salt and ground black pepper

1 Place the potatoes in a large pan. Cover with cold water and bring to the boil. Cook for 10–15 minutes, or until they are only just tender.

VARIATIONS

• For a speedy version of these individual pies, buy ready-prepared potato rösti and sprinkle it evenly over the fish and sauce as in step 6.
• To make an alternative topping, cook the potatoes until soft, drain and mash with a little milk and butter. Spoon the mashed potato over the fish and sauce and top with cheese as in step 6.
• Add 30ml/2 tbsp chopped capers to the sauce at the end of step 5.

2 Drain the potatoes well, and set aside until they are cool enough to handle. Peel and coarsely grate the par-boiled potatoes into a large mixing bowl. Stir in the melted butter and season well with salt and pepper.

3 Preheat the oven to 220°C/425°F/ Gas 7. Divide the pieces of cod or haddock and the prawns, mussels and scallops among four individual 19cm/ 7½in rectangular earthenware dishes.

4 Melt the butter in a large pan, add the onion and cook for 6–8 minutes, stirring occasionally with a wooden spoon, or until softened and light golden. Sprinkle in the flour and stir thoroughly with a wooden spoon until well blended.

5 Remove the pan from the heat and gradually pour in the wine and stock, stirring constantly until smooth. Bring to the boil, stirring constantly, then stir in the cream, dill and parsley and season to taste. Pour the sauce over the fish.

6 Sprinkle the grated potato evenly over the fish and sauce in the dishes and top with the grated Parmesan cheese. Bake for 25 minutes, or until the topping is crisp and golden and the fish is cooked. Serve hot, garnished with dill.

COOK'S TIP

Choose waxy potatoes for this dish and cook until barely tender. Floury potatoes are too soft and will break up, so if you only have floury potatoes, opt for the mashed potato option (see Variations).

SHELLFISH TAGINE

*The distinctive mixture of spices and chillies used in this tagine is known as charmoula –
a classic Moroccan marinade for fish, meat and vegetable dishes.*

SERVES 4

60ml/4 tbsp olive oil
4 garlic cloves, sliced
1–2 green chillies, seeded and chopped
a large handful of flat leaf parsley,
    roughly chopped
5ml/1 tsp coriander seeds
2.5ml/½ tsp ground allspice
6 cardamom pods, split open
2.5ml/½ tsp ground turmeric
15ml/1 tbsp lemon juice
350g/12oz scorpion fish, red mullet or red
    snapper fillets, cut into large chunks
225g/8oz squid, cleaned and cut into rings
1 onion, chopped
4 tomatoes, seeded and chopped
300ml/½ pint/1¼ cups warm fish or
    vegetable stock
225g/8oz large, raw prawns (shrimp)
15ml/1 tbsp chopped fresh
    coriander (cilantro)
salt and ground black pepper
lemon wedges, to garnish
couscous or rice and crusty bread,
    to serve

1 Place the olive oil, garlic, chillies,
parsley, coriander seeds, allspice and
cardamom pods in a mortar and pound
to a smooth paste using a pestle. Stir in
the ground turmeric, salt, pepper and
lemon juice.

VARIATIONS

Scorpion fish is the traditional choice for
this dish and red mullet or snapper makes
a good, authentic alternative, but there's
no reason why you shouldn't substitute
other fish – try red bream, porgy or even
halved cod or hake steaks.

2 Place the chunks of fish in a large glass
or china bowl with the squid rings, add
the spice paste and toss together. Cover
and leave the fish to marinate in the
refrigerator for about 2 hours, or longer,
if time allows.

3 Place the chopped onion, seeded and
chopped tomatoes and fish or vegetable
stock in a tagine (see Cook's Tip) and
cover. Place the tagine in an unheated
oven and set the oven to 200°C/400°F/
Gas 6. Cook the vegetables for 20 minutes.

4 Remove the fish from the marinade,
then drain well. Set aside the squid and
any excess marinade, then place the fish
in the tagine with the vegetables. Cover
and cook in the oven for 5 minutes.

5 Add the prawns, squid rings and the
remaining marinade to the tagine and stir
to combine. Cover the tagine and return
it to the oven for 5–10 minutes, or until
all the fish, prawns and squid are cooked
right through.

6 Taste the sauce and season to taste
with salt and pepper if necessary, then
stir in the chopped coriander. Serve
immediately, garnished with lemon
wedges. Serve the tagine with couscous
or rice and crusty bread to soak up
the juices.

COOK'S TIPS

• A tagine is a traditional Moroccan stew
and it is also the name given to the
shallow earthenware cooking dish with a
tall, conical, earthenware lid in which the
stew is traditionally cooked. A shallow,
earthenware baking dish or a soaked,
shallow clay pot can be used in place of
a tagine.
• To ensure that the fish fillets have no
tiny bones left in the flesh after filleting,
lay the fillets on a board, skin-side down,
and run your hand gently over the surface
of the flesh. Pull out any bones that you
find using a pair of tweezers.

VEGETARIAN MAIN MEALS

Coming home to a delectable slow-cooked dish is always a delight. You open the door to delicious, tantalizing smells, take a few moments to assemble plates and cutlery, and tuck in. On occasions like these, a vegetarian dish such as Moroccan Braised Chickpeas is the ideal choice, or try Clay-pot Risotto with Spinach and Saffron or Vegetable Paella. The steamy atmosphere inside the pot creates the perfect cooking environment.

TOMATO, FETA CHEESE and OLIVE TARTS

These upside-down tartlets are filled with vegetables and chunks of salty cheese. They make the perfect first course, or may be served with salad leaves for a lunchtime snack.

SERVES 4

25g/1oz sun-dried aubergine
   (eggplant) slices
300ml/½ pint/1¼ cups boiling water
45ml/3 tbsp sunflower oil
1 onion, thinly sliced
150g/5oz/2 cups button (white)
   mushrooms, sliced
1 garlic clove, crushed
12–16 cherry tomatoes, halved
8 black or green olives, pitted
   and chopped
115g/4oz/1 cup feta cheese, crumbled
350g/12oz ready-made puff pastry
salt and ground black pepper

1 Preheat the oven to 200°C/400°F/ Gas 6. Place the aubergine slices in a shallow dish. Pour over the boiling water and leave to soak for 10 minutes. Rinse in cold water, drain and dry on kitchen paper. Cut the aubergine slices in half or quarters, depending on their size.

2 Heat 30ml/2 tbsp of the sunflower oil in a frying pan and fry the onion over a medium heat for 4–5 minutes. Add the mushrooms and cook for 3–4 minutes, or until the onions are light golden. Remove and set aside.

3 Heat the remaining oil in the frying pan, add the aubergine slices and garlic and lightly fry for 1–2 minutes. Lightly oil four individual cazuelas. Mix the halved tomatoes with the onions, mushrooms, aubergines, olives and feta cheese and divide among the cazuelas. Season well.

4 Roll out the pastry thinly into an oblong, then cut out four rounds, each slightly larger than the diameter of the cazuelas. Place the pastry on top of the vegetable and cheese mixture, tucking the overlap down inside the dish.

5 Bake for 20 minutes, or until the pastry is risen and golden. Cool slightly then invert on to individual warmed serving plates to serve.

COOK'S TIP
Choose cherry tomatoes on the vine for the very best flavour.

LENTIL FRITTATA

Throughout the Mediterranean a variety of thick, vegetable omelettes are cooked. This tasty supper dish combines green lentils, red onions, broccoli and cherry tomatoes.

SERVES 4–6

75g/3oz/scant ½ cup green lentils
225g/8oz small broccoli florets
2 red onions, halved and thickly sliced
30ml/2 tbsp olive oil
8 eggs
45ml/3 tbsp milk or water
45ml/3 tbsp chopped mixed herbs, such as
    oregano, parsley, tarragon and chives,
    plus extra sprigs to garnish
175g/6oz cherry tomatoes, halved
salt and ground black pepper

1 Place the lentils in a pan, cover with cold water and bring to the boil, reduce the heat and simmer for 25 minutes until tender. Add the broccoli, return to the boil and cook for 1 minute.

VARIATIONS

Add about 50g/2oz/⅔ cup freshly grated Parmesan cheese or 115g/4oz/1 cup diced mozzarella cheese to the egg mixture.

2 Meanwhile place the onion slices and olive oil in a shallow earthenware dish or cazuela about 23–25cm/9–10in in diameter and place in an unheated oven. Set the oven to 200°C/400°F/Gas 6 and cook for 25 minutes.

3 In a bowl, whisk together the eggs, milk or water, a pinch of salt and plenty of black pepper. Stir in the herbs. Drain the lentils and broccoli and stir into the onions. Add the cherry tomatoes. Stir gently to combine.

4 Pour the egg mixture evenly over the vegetables. Reduce the oven to 190°C/375°F/Gas 5. Return the dish to the oven and cook for 10 minutes, then push the mixture into the centre of the dish using a spatula, allowing the raw mixture in the centre to flow to the edges.

5 Return the dish to the oven and cook the frittata for a further 15 minutes, or until it is just set. Garnish with sprigs of fresh herbs and serve warm, cut into thick wedges.

TAGLIATELLE BAKED with MUSHROOMS, GORGONZOLA and WALNUTS

This rich, creamy dish is perfect served as a lunch or supper dish with a mixed leaf salad.

2 Meanwhile, place the tagliatelle in a large pan of boiling salted water and cook according to packet instructions or until just tender.

3 Remove the mushrooms and leeks and set aside. Crumble the Gorgonzola cheese into the frying pan and stir over a gentle heat, until melted. Stir in the creams and the dry vermouth or white wine and season to taste.

SERVES 4

25g/1oz/2 tbsp butter
15ml/1 tbsp vegetable oil
350g/12oz/4 cups chestnut mushrooms, quartered, or brown cap (crimini) mushrooms, halved
2 leeks, thinly sliced
400g/14oz mixed spinach and plain tagliatelle
175g/6oz Gorgonzola cheese
150ml/¼ pint/⅔ cup double (heavy) cream
200ml/7fl oz/scant 1 cup thick single (light) cream
90ml/6 tbsp dry vermouth or white wine
50g/2oz/½ cup walnuts, finely chopped
75g/3oz/1 cup grated Parmesan cheese
salt and ground black pepper

1 Preheat the oven to 200°C/400°F/ Gas 6. Melt the butter with the oil in a large sauté pan or deep frying pan, add the quartered chestnut mushrooms or halved brown cap mushrooms and the thinly sliced leeks and stir-fry the vegetables together for 4–5 minutes.

4 Drain the pasta and divide it among four individual cazuelas or other shallow ovenproof earthenware dishes. Top with the mushrooms and leeks, spreading them over the pasta. Pour over the sauce, sprinkle the chopped walnuts and Parmesan cheese on top and bake for about 15 minutes, or until the cheese is golden brown and bubbling.

VARIATION
Any type of pasta shapes can be used in this bake in place of the tagliatelle. However, other long ribbon pastas, such as linguine and bucatini, and hollow tube pastas that scoop up the sauce, such as macaroni, penne or rigatoni, will work particularly well.

MOROCCAN BRAISED CHICKPEAS

This sweet and spicy vegetarian dish is a real treat. Serve it hot as a main course with rice or couscous or serve cold as a salad, drizzled with olive oil and lemon juice.

SERVES 4

250g/9oz/1½ cups dried chickpeas, soaked
    overnight in cold water
30ml/2 tbsp olive oil
2 onions, cut into wedges
10ml/2 tsp ground cumin
1.5ml/¼ tsp ground turmeric
1.5ml/¼ tsp cayenne pepper
15ml/1 tbsp ground coriander
5ml/1 tsp ground cinnamon
300ml/½ pint/1¼ cups vegetable stock
2 carrots, sliced
115g/4oz/½ cup ready-to-eat dried
    apricots, halved
50g/2oz/scant ½ cup raisins
25g/1oz/¼ cup flaked (sliced) almonds
30ml/2 tbsp chopped fresh
    coriander (cilantro)
30ml/2 tbsp chopped fresh flat leaf parsley
salt and ground black pepper

3 Meanwhile, place the olive oil and onions in a frying pan and cook for about 6 minutes, or until softened. Add the cumin, turmeric, cayenne, coriander and cinnamon and cook for 2–3 minutes. Stir in the stock, carrots, apricots, raisins and almonds and bring to the boil.

4 Drain the chickpeas, add the spicy vegetable mixture and stir. Cover and return to the oven for 30 minutes.

5 Season with salt and pepper, lightly stir in half the fresh coriander and parsley and serve sprinkled with the remainder.

1 Soak a bean clay pot in cold water for 20 minutes, then drain. Place the chickpeas in a pan with plenty of cold water. Bring to the boil and boil rapidly for 10 minutes, then place the chickpeas in the bean pot, cover with lukewarm water and cover.

2 Place in an unheated oven and set the temperature to 200°C/400°F/Gas 6. Cook for 1 hour, then reduce the oven temperature to 160°C/325°/Gas 3. Cook for another hour, or until the chickpeas are tender.

COOK'S TIP
The cooking time for the chickpeas will vary depending on their age – if old, they could take a further 30 minutes.

MIXED BEAN and AUBERGINE TAGINE with MINT YOGURT

In this traditional-style Moroccan dish, the mixed beans and aubergine provide both texture and flavour, which are enhanced by the herbs and chillies.

SERVES 4

115g/4oz/generous ½ cup dried red kidney beans, soaked overnight in cold water and drained
115g/4oz/generous ½ cup dried black-eyed beans (peas) or cannellini beans, soaked overnight in cold water and drained
600ml/1 pint/2½ cups water
2 bay leaves
2 celery sticks, each cut into 4 batons
75ml/5 tbsp olive oil
1 aubergine (eggplant), about 350g/12oz, cut into chunks
1 onion, thinly sliced
3 garlic cloves, crushed
1–2 fresh red chillies, seeded and finely chopped
30ml/2 tbsp tomato purée (paste)
5ml/1 tsp paprika
2 large tomatoes, roughly chopped
300ml/½ pint/1¼ cups vegetable stock
15ml/1 tbsp each chopped fresh mint, parsley and coriander (cilantro)
salt and ground black pepper
fresh herb sprigs, to garnish

For the mint yogurt
150ml/¼ pint/⅔ cup natural (plain) yogurt
30ml/2 tbsp chopped fresh mint
2 spring onions (scallions), chopped

1 Place the soaked and drained kidney beans in a large pan of unsalted boiling water. Bring back to the boil and boil rapidly for 10 minutes, then drain. Place the soaked and drained black-eyed or cannellini beans in a separate large pan of boiling unsalted water and boil rapidly for 10 minutes, then drain.

2 Place the 600ml/1 pint/2½ cups of water in a soaked bean pot or a large tagine, add the bay leaves, celery and beans. Cover and place in an unheated oven. Set the oven to 190°C/375°F/Gas 5. Cook for 1–1½ hours or until the beans are tender. Drain.

3 Heat 60ml/4 tbsp of the oil in a large frying pan or cast-iron tagine base. Add the aubergine chunks and cook, stirring for 4–5 minutes, until evenly browned. Remove and set aside.

4 Add the remaining oil to the tagine base or frying pan, then add the onion and cook, stirring, for 4–5 minutes, until softened. Add the garlic and chillies and cook for a further 5 minutes, stirring frequently, until the onion is golden.

VARIATIONS
• Use 10–15ml/2–3 tsp harissa paste or chilli sauce instead of fresh chillies.
• A mixture of courgettes (zucchini) and red and yellow (bell) peppers can be used instead of the aubergines. Cut them into small chunks and fry them in the oil as in step 3 above.

5 Reduce the oven temperature to 160°C/325°F/Gas 3. Add the tomato purée and paprika and cook, stirring, for 1–2 minutes. Add the tomatoes, browned aubergine, drained red kidney and black-eyed or cannellini beans and stock. Season with salt and pepper.

6 Cover the iron tagine base with the earthenware lid or, if using a frying pan, transfer the contents to a clay tagine. Place in the oven and cook for 1 hour.

7 Meanwhile, mix together the yogurt, mint and spring onions and place in a small serving dish. To serve, add the mint, parsley and coriander to the tagine and lightly mix through the vegetables. Season to taste. Garnish with fresh herb sprigs and serve with the mint yogurt.

COOK'S TIP
The cooking time for the dried beans will vary depending on the age of the beans. Older beans will take longer to cook until tender. The tagine will happily keep warm once it's ready, so if you are serving this to guests, it is a good idea to allow extra time for the beans to become tender.

ROASTED SQUASH with RICE STUFFING

Gem squash has a sweet, subtle taste that contrasts well with the olives and sun-dried tomatoes in this recipe. The rice adds substance without changing any of the flavour.

SERVES 4 AS A FIRST COURSE

4 whole gem squashes
225g/8oz cooked white long grain rice
    (about 90g/3½oz/½ cup raw weight)
75g/3oz sun-dried tomatoes in oil, drained
    and chopped
50g/2oz/½ cup pitted black olives, chopped
60ml/4 tbsp soft goat's cheese
30ml/2 tbsp olive oil
15ml/1 tbsp chopped fresh basil leaves,
    plus basil sprigs, to serve
yogurt and mint dressing and green salad,
    to serve

1 Preheat the oven to 180°C/350°F/ Gas 4. Using a sharp knife, trim the base of each squash, slice off the top of each and scoop out and discard the seeds.

2 Mix the rice, tomatoes, olives, cheese, half the oil and the basil in a bowl.

3 Oil a shallow baking dish with the remaining oil, just large enough to hold the squash side by side. Divide the rice mixture among the squash and place them in the dish.

4 Cover with foil and bake for about 45 minutes until the squash are tender when pierced with a skewer. Garnish with basil sprigs and serve with a yogurt and mint dressing and a green salad.

VARIATION
Try ricotta cheese or cream cheese with garlic and herbs in place of the soft goat's cheese in this recipe.

CLAY-POT RISOTTO with SPINACH and SAFFRON

Rice cooks to perfection in the moist environment of a clay pot. This risotto can be made without the constant checking required when cooked on top of the stove.

SERVES 4

a few saffron threads
30ml/2 tbsp boiling water
15ml/1 tbsp olive oil
50g/2oz/¼ cup butter
1 onion, finely chopped
350g/12oz/1¾ cups risotto rice
900ml/1½ pints/3¾ cups warm
 vegetable stock
150ml/¼ pint/⅔ cup dry white wine
225g/8oz baby spinach leaves
300ml/½ pint/1¼ cups hot vegetable stock
40g/1½oz/¼ cup shelled walnuts, chopped
75g/3oz Parmesan cheese, very
 finely shaved
salt and ground black pepper

1 Soak a large clay pot in cold water for 20 minutes, then drain. Meanwhile, place the saffron in a bowl, cover with the boiling water and leave to infuse (steep).

2 Heat the oil and half the butter in a large, heavy pan. Add the finely chopped onion and cook gently for 5 minutes, or until soft, stirring occasionally. Add the rice and stir over the heat for about 3 minutes until the grains are thoroughly coated in oil and butter.

COOK'S TIP
Risotto rice is short grain rice that is widely used in Italy to make a variety of different types of risotto. Arborio rice is the most widely available type, but you may also find carnaroli and vialone nano. When cooked, risotto rice has a creamy consistency but the grains retain a slight "bite" to their texture.

3 Pour the warm stock into the clay pot, add the saffron water, wine and the rice mixture and stir together. Cover and place in an unheated oven. Set the oven to 190°C/375°F/Gas 5 and cook for 50 minutes, stirring after 30 minutes.

4 Stir in the spinach, add the stock, then cover and cook for 10 minutes, or until the rice is tender. Stir in the walnuts, the remaining butter and half the Parmesan cheese. Season and serve sprinkled with the remaining Parmesan cheese.

VEGETABLE PAELLA

A colourful assortment of vegetables is cooked slowly with rice to make this tasty – slightly spicy – vegetarian meal.

SERVES 4

1 large aubergine (eggplant)
45ml/3 tbsp extra virgin olive or
   sunflower oil
2 onions, quartered and sliced
2 garlic cloves, crushed
300g/11oz/1½ cups short grain Spanish or
   risotto rice
1.2–1.5 litres/2–2½ pints/5–6¼ cups
   vegetable stock
1 red (bell) pepper, halved, seeded
   and sliced
1 yellow (bell) pepper, halved, seeded
   and sliced
200g/7oz fine green beans, halved
115g/4oz/scant 2 cups chestnut
   mushrooms, quartered, or brown
   cap (cremini) or button (white)
   mushrooms, halved
1 dried chilli, crushed
115g/4oz/1 cup frozen peas
salt and ground black pepper
fresh coriander (cilantro) leaves,
   to garnish

2 Heat 30ml/2 tbsp of the oil in a large frying pan, add the aubergine slices and quickly sauté until slightly golden. Transfer to the clay pot.

3 Add the remaining oil, add the onion and cook, stirring occasionally, for a few minutes until golden.

4 Add the garlic and rice and cook for 1–2 minutes, stirring, until the rice becomes transparent. Pour in 900ml/ 1½ pints/3¾ cups of the stock into the clay pot, then add the rice mixture.

5 Add the peppers, halved green beans, mushrooms, crushed chilli and seasoning. Stir to mix, then cover the pot and place in an unheated oven.

6 Set the oven to 200°C/400°F/Gas 6 and cook for 1 hour, or until the rice is almost tender. After 40 minutes, remove the pot from the oven and add a little more stock to moisten the paella. Stir well, re-cover and return to the oven.

7 Add the peas and a little more stock to the paella and cook for a further 10 minutes. Adjust the seasoning and sprinkle over the coriander. Lightly stir through and then serve.

VARIATIONS
• Almost any roughly chopped or sliced vegetables can be used in this dish. Broccoli, carrots, cauliflower, courgettes (zucchini) and okra are all suitable – or try using frozen sweetcorn in place of all or some of the peas.
• For a tomato-flavoured paella, use a 400g/14oz can chopped tomatoes in place of 350ml/12floz/1½ cups of the stock.

1 Soak a clay pot or Chinese sand pot in cold water for 20 minutes, then drain. Cut the aubergine in half lengthwise, then cut it crosswise into thin slices.

COOK'S TIP
Although nowadays aubergines don't need to be salted to remove the bitter flavour they used to have, salting them does ensure that they absorb less oil when they are fried. So, if you have the time, layer the slices in a colander and sprinkle each layer with salt. Leave the slices to drain for about 30 minutes, then rinse thoroughly and pat dry before frying.

BULGUR WHEAT, ASPARAGUS and BROAD BEAN PILAFF

Nutty-textured bulgur wheat is usually simply soaked in boiling water until it is softened, but it can be cooked like rice to make a pilaff. Here it is combined with broad beans, herbs and lemon and orange rinds, which add a fresh, springtime flavour.

SERVES 4

250g/9oz/1½ cups bulgur wheat
750–900ml/1¼–1½ pints/3–3¾ cups warm
    vegetable stock
225g/8oz asparagus spears
225g/8oz/2 cups frozen broad (fava)
    beans, thawed
8 spring onions (scallions), chopped
15ml/1 tbsp grated lemon rind
15ml/1 tbsp grated orange rind
40g/1½oz/3 tbsp butter, cut into
    small pieces
60ml/4 tbsp chopped fresh flat leaf parsley
30ml/2 tbsp chopped fresh dill, plus extra
    sprigs to garnish
salt and ground black pepper

1 If using a clay pot, soak in cold water for 20 minutes, then drain. Place the bulgur wheat in the clay pot or in a shallow, ovenproof earthenware dish and pour over 600ml/1 pint/2½ cups of the stock. Season with salt and pepper.

VARIATIONS

• Try using fresh green beans and either fresh or frozen peas in place of the asparagus and broad beans and, instead of using dill, stir in plenty of chopped fresh mint along with the parsley.
• If you'd like to add a little extra colour to the pilaff, then stir in some finely shredded red (bell) pepper, or some peeled and seeded wedges of tomato.
• To make a richer pilaff, stir in some finely grated Parmesan cheese along with the butter in step 6.

2 Cut the asparagus spears into 2.5cm/1in lengths, discarding any hard, woody ends from the stems. Add the asparagus pieces to the clay pot or dish and gently stir these into the bulgur wheat.

3 Cover the clay pot or dish tightly and place in an unheated oven. Set the oven to 200°C/400°F/Gas 6 and then cook the bulgur wheat and asparagus for 20 minutes.

4 Meanwhile pop the broad beans out of their shells and then stir the beans into the bulgur pilaff after it has cooked for about 20 minutes, adding a little more stock at the same time. Re-cover the clay pot or dish and return the dish to the oven for about 10 minutes.

COOK'S TIP

If your clay pot or earthenware dish doesn't have its own lid, then cover the pot or dish with foil, crimping it around the edge to seal. Or, if the top of the dish is completely flat, then you can simply place a flat, heavy baking sheet on top.

5 Stir in the spring onions, grated lemon and orange rind. Add a little more stock, if necessary. Cover and return to the oven for 5 minutes.

6 Dot the pieces of butter over the top of the pilaff and leave to stand, covered, for 5 minutes.

7 Add the chopped parsley and dill to the pilaff and stir well with a fork, to fluff up the bulgur wheat and distribute the herbs evenly. Check the seasoning and add salt and plenty of black pepper. Serve the pilaff hot, garnished with sprigs of fresh dill.

VEGETABLE
SIDE DISHES

With the modern emphasis on eating plenty of
vegetables, serving several side dishes makes sense,
but it can present logistical problems. Space on
top of the stove is often limited, so use the oven
as well. Choose something quick and simple, such
as Braised Red Cabbage with Beetroot or New
Potatoes with Thyme and Lemon. Or go for a dish
that's a little more out of the ordinary, such as
Field Mushrooms with Hazelnuts.

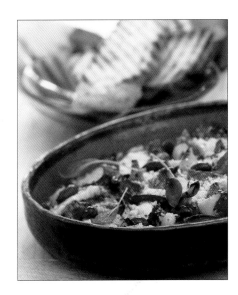

BRAISED RED CABBAGE with BEETROOT

The moist, gentle cooking of the clay pot finishes this vegetable dish to perfection.
Serve with casseroles and roast meats – it is especially delicious with roast pork.

SERVES 6–8

675g/1½lb red cabbage
1 Spanish onion, thinly sliced
30ml/2 tbsp olive oil
30ml/2 tbsp light muscovado (brown) sugar
2 tart eating apples, peeled, cored
    and sliced
300ml/½ pint/1¼ cups vegetable stock
60ml/4 tbsp red wine vinegar
375g/13oz raw beetroot (beet), peeled
    and coarsely grated
salt and ground black pepper

COOK'S TIP
When buying cabbage, choose one that
is firm and heavy for its size. The leaves
should look healthy – avoid any with
curling leaves or blemishes. These
guidelines apply to any type of cabbage –
red, green or white.

1 Soak a large clay pot or bean pot in
cold water for 20 minutes, then drain.
Finely shred the red cabbage and place
in the clay pot.

2 Place the onion and olive oil in a
frying pan and sauté until soft and
transparent. Stir in the sugar and fry the
onion gently until it is caramelized and
golden. Take care not to overcook.

3 Stir in the apple slices, vegetable stock
and wine vinegar, then transfer to the
clay pot. Season with salt and pepper.

4 Cover and place in an unheated oven.
Set the oven temperature to 190°C/
375°F/Gas 5 and cook for 1 hour. Stir in
the beetroot, re-cover the pot and cook
for a further 20–30 minutes, or until the
cabbage and beetroot are tender.

NEW POTATOES with THYME and LEMON

These potatoes are the perfect accompaniment to meat or poultry. You can even use old potatoes, cut into chunks, ideal for serving as an alternative with a traditional roast.

SERVES 4

675g/1½lb small new potatoes
4 garlic cloves, sliced
8 thyme sprigs
4 strips finely pared lemon rind
75ml/5 tbsp olive oil
coarsely ground black pepper
coarse sea salt

COOK'S TIPS
• Thyme is an aromatic, woody herb that goes particularly well with lemon. It has a strong aroma and pungent flavour and grows wild in most warm climates. Thyme is often associated with dishes from the Mediterranean.
• You could easily make this dish with older potatoes – simply peel them, if you like, then cut them into even-size chunks or wedges before adding them to the pot.

1 Soak a clay potato pot in cold water for 20 minutes, then drain. Scrub the new potatoes and rinse thoroughly in cold water. Place the potatoes in the pot.

2 Add the sliced garlic cloves, thyme sprigs and pared lemon rind to the pot, tucking them in among the potatoes. Sprinkle over plenty of coarsely ground black pepper and coarse sea salt.

3 Drizzle over the olive oil. Cover with the lid and place in an unheated oven. Set the oven to 200°C/400°F/Gas 6 and cook for 1 hour, or until just tender.

4 If wished, remove the lid and bake for a further 15–20 minutes, until slightly golden. If you prefer to keep the skins soft, remove the potatoes from the oven and leave to stand for 10 minutes.

POTATOES and PARSNIPS BAKED with GARLIC and CREAM

As the potatoes and parsnips cook, they gradually absorb the garlic-flavoured cream, while the cheese browns to a crispy finish.

SERVES 4–6

3 large potatoes, total weight about
　675g/1½lb
350g/12oz small to medium parsnips
200ml/7fl oz/scant 1 cup single
　(light) cream
105ml/7 tbsp milk
2 garlic cloves, crushed
butter, for greasing
about 5ml/1 tsp freshly grated nutmeg
75g/3oz/¾ cup coarsely grated
　Gruyère cheese
salt and ground black pepper

3 Lightly grease a 25cm/10in rectangular earthenware baking dish. Preheat the oven to 180°C/350°F/Gas 4.

1 Peel the potatoes and parsnips and cut them into thin slices using a sharp knife. Place them in a large pan of salted boiling water and cook for 5 minutes. Drain and leave to cool slightly.

2 Meanwhile, pour the cream and milk into a heavy pan, add the crushed garlic and bring to the boil over a medium heat. Remove the pan from the heat and leave to stand at room temperature for about 10 minutes to allow the flavour of the garlic to infuse into the cream and milk mixture.

4 Arrange the potatoes and parsnips in layers in the greased earthenware dish, sprinkling each layer with a little freshly grated nutmeg and plenty of salt and ground black pepper.

5 Pour the garlic-flavoured cream and milk mixture into the dish and then press the sliced potatoes and parsnips down into the liquid. The liquid should come to just underneath the top layer of vegetables. Cover the dish with a piece of lightly buttered foil or baking parchment and bake for 45 minutes.

6 Remove the dish from the oven and remove the foil or parchment from the dish. Sprinkle the grated Gruyère cheese over the vegetables in an even layer.

7 Return the dish to the oven and bake uncovered for a further 20–30 minutes, or until the potatoes and parsnips are tender (see Cook's Tip) and the topping is golden brown.

COOK'S TIPS

• If you have one, use a mandolin or a food processor fitted with a slicing blade to thinly and evenly slice the potatoes and parsnips for this gratin.
• At the end of the cooking time, to test if the vegetables are tender, insert a sharp knife through the middle of the potatoes and parsnips. The knife should slide in easily and the vegetables feel soft.

VARIATIONS

• Use sweet potatoes in place of some or all of the ordinary potatoes – choose orange-fleshed ones for a pretty colour contrast with the parsnips. Other root vegetables such as Jerusalem artichokes and carrots would also work well.
• Other hard cheeses would be equally good in this recipe – try Cheddar or Red Leicester, or go for the even more strongly flavoured Parmesan or Pecorino.

FIELD MUSHROOMS with HAZELNUTS

Large mushrooms, full of texture and flavour, are topped with crunchy hazelnut pieces and fresh parsley and garlic-flavoured olive oil.

SERVES 4

2 garlic cloves
grated rind of 1 lemon
90ml/6 tbsp olive oil
8 large field (portabello) mushrooms
50g/2oz/½ cup hazelnuts, coarsely chopped
30ml/2 tbsp chopped fresh parsley
salt and ground black pepper

1 Crush the garlic cloves with a little salt using a mortar and pestle or on a chopping board. Place the crushed garlic in a small bowl and stir in the grated lemon rind and the olive oil. If time allows, leave the mixture to stand to enable the flavours to infuse (steep).

2 Preheat the oven to 200°C/400°F/ Gas 6. Arrange the mushrooms, stalk side up, in a single layer in an ovenproof earthenware dish. Drizzle over about 60ml/4 tbsp of the oil mixture and bake for 10 minutes.

3 Remove the mushrooms from the oven and baste them with the remaining oil mixture, then sprinkle the chopped hazelnuts evenly over the top. Bake for a further 10–15 minutes, or until the mushrooms are tender. Season with salt and pepper and sprinkle with chopped parsley. Serve immediately.

COOK'S TIP
Almost any unsalted nuts can be used in place of the hazelnuts in this recipe – try pine nuts, cashew nuts, almonds or walnuts. Nuts can go rancid quickly so, for the freshest flavour, either buy nuts in small quantities or buy them in shells and remove the shells just before use.

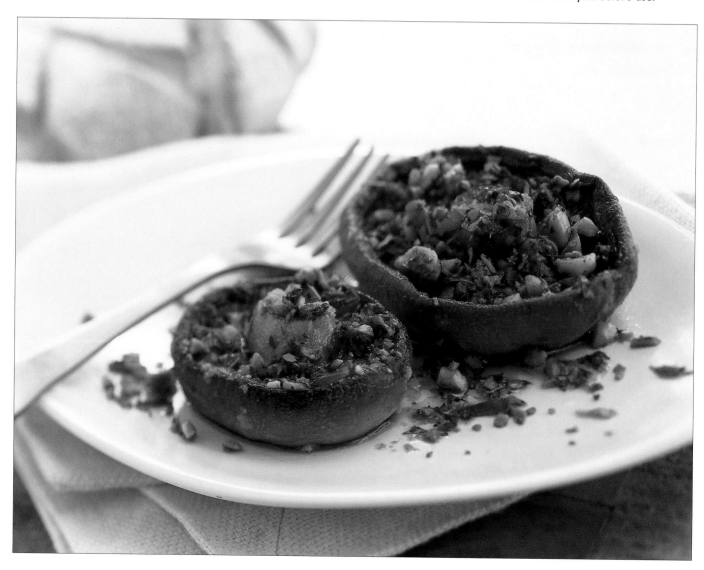

MEDITERRANEAN BAKED VEGETABLES

This colourful selection of vegetables is baked in a shallow clay pot, known as a tian *in Provence where it is also the name given to the food baked in it.*

SERVES 4–6

75ml/5 tbsp olive oil
2 onions, halved and sliced
1 garlic clove, crushed
15ml/1 tbsp finely chopped
    fresh sage
4 large, well-flavoured
    tomatoes, quartered
3 courgettes (zucchini),
    thickly sliced
2 small yellow (bell) peppers, quartered
    and seeded
2 small red (bell) peppers, quartered
    and seeded
60ml/4 tbsp fresh white or wholemeal
    (whole-wheat) breadcrumbs
60ml/4 tbsp freshly grated
    Parmesan cheese
8–10 pitted black olives
salt and ground black pepper
sage leaves, to garnish

1 Heat 30ml/2 tbsp of the olive oil in a frying pan, add the onions and cook, stirring occasionally, until softened. Add the garlic and continue cooking until the onions are really soft and golden. Stir in the sage and season well.

2 Transfer the onions to a large oval *tian* or earthenware baking dish. Spread them evenly, then arrange the tomatoes, courgettes and peppers on top.

3 Preheat the oven to 200°F/400°C/ Gas 6. Drizzle the remaining oil over the mixed vegetables and season well. Bake for 30 minutes.

4 Sprinkle the fresh breadcrumbs and Parmesan cheese over the vegetables and arrange the olives on top. Return to the oven for a further 10–15 minutes, or until the vegetables are tender. Serve garnished with the sage leaves.

DESSERTS

The clever cook who saves time and effort by mastering clay-pot cooking deserves a sweet reward, and what better way to celebrate succcess than with Baked Maple and Pecan Croissant Pudding or Honey-baked Figs – cooked in a clay pot, of course – served with Hazelnut Ice Cream. Strawberry Oat Crunch is another treat or, for pots of pleasure, try sweet and tangy Spiced Pears with Nut Crumble or elegant and impressive Nectarines Baked with Almonds and Pistachio Nuts.

  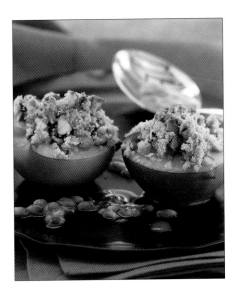

PLUM CHARLOTTES with FOAMY KIRSCH SAUCE

*These individual puddings, cooked in mini earthenware dishes, conceal a fresh plum filling
and are served on a pool of light, frothy Kirsch-flavoured sauce.*

SERVES 4

115g/4oz/½ cup butter, melted
50g/2oz/4 tbsp demerara (raw) sugar
450g/1lb ripe plums, stoned (pitted) and
    thickly sliced
25g/1oz/2 tbsp caster (superfine) sugar
30ml/2 tbsp water
1.5ml/¼ tsp ground cinnamon
25g/1oz/¼ cup ground almonds
8–10 large slices of white bread

For the Kirsch sauce

3 egg yolks
40g/1½oz/3 tbsp caster
    (superfine) sugar
30ml/2 tbsp Kirsch

2 Place the stoned plum slices in a pan
with the caster sugar, water and ground
cinnamon and cook gently for 5 minutes,
or until the plums have softened slightly.
Leave them to cool, then stir in the
ground almonds.

5 Divide the plum mixture among the
lined dishes. Place the bread rounds on
top and brush with the remaining butter.
Place the ramekins on a baking sheet
and bake for 25 minutes.

1 Preheat the oven to 190°C/375°F/
Gas 5. Line the base of four individual
10cm/4in-diameter deep, earthenware
ramekin dishes with baking parchment.
Brush evenly and thoroughly with a little
of the melted butter, then sprinkle each
dish with a little of the demerara sugar,
rotating the dish in your hands to coat
each dish evenly.

VARIATIONS

• Slices of peeled pear or eating apples
can be used in this recipe instead of the
stoned, sliced plums.
• If using apples or pears substitute the
Kirsch in the foamy sauce with Calvados
or another apple brandy.
• If you are short on time, drained canned
fruit such as pineapple, apricots, pears or
plums can be used – simply stir in the
ground almonds as in step 2 and add to
the prepared ramekins.

3 Cut the crusts off the bread and then
use a plain pastry cutter to cut out four
rounds to fit the bases of the ramekins.
Dip the bread rounds into the melted
butter and fit them into the dishes. Cut
four more rounds to fit the tops of the
dishes and set aside.

4 Cut the remaining bread into strips,
dip into the melted butter and use to
line the sides of the ramekins completely.

6 Just before the charlottes are ready
place the egg yolks and caster sugar for
the sauce in a bowl. Whisk together
until pale. Place the bowl over a pan of
simmering water and whisk in the Kirsch.
Continue whisking until the mixture is
very light and frothy.

7 Remove the charlottes from the oven
and turn out on to warm serving plates.
Pour a little sauce over and around the
charlottes and serve immediately.

COOK'S TIP

For an extra indulgent dessert, serve the
puddings with lightly whipped double
(heavy) cream flavoured with extra Kirsch
and sweetened to taste with a little
sieved icing (confectioners') sugar.

SPICED PEARS with NUT CRUMBLE

An all-time favourite, this crumble has a crunchy pecan nut and oat topping,
which complements the spicy pears hidden beneath.

SERVES 4–6

900g/2lb pears
30ml/2 tbsp lemon juice
40g/1½oz/3 tbsp caster (superfine) sugar
5ml/1 tsp mixed (apple pie) spice
2.5ml/½ tsp grated nutmeg
vanilla ice cream, to serve

For the crumble topping
75g/3oz/⅔ cup plain (all-purpose) flour
75g/3oz/6 tbsp butter
50g/2oz/¼ cup light muscovado
    (brown) sugar
50g/2oz/½ cup pecan nuts or
    walnuts, chopped
40g/1½oz/scant ½ cup rolled oats

COOK'S TIP
Look out for golden-skinned Forelle pears, which are especially good for cooking, or try Anjou, Williams or Conference pears.

1 Soak a small clay pot in cold water for 15 minutes, then drain. Peel the pears if wished, then halve them and remove the cores. Cut each pear into six wedges and toss in the lemon juice.

2 Place the pears in the clay pot, add the sugar, mixed spice and nutmeg and mix together. Place in an unheated oven, set the oven to 200°C/400°F/Gas 6 and cook for 25 minutes.

3 Meanwhile, prepare the crumble topping. Sift the flour into a bowl and rub in the butter, then stir in the sugar, nuts and rolled oats.

4 Uncover the clay pot and stir gently to rearrange the fruit. Spoon the crumble mixture over the pears, then return the clay pot to the oven for 25–30 minutes, or until the crumble is golden. Serve warm, with vanilla ice cream.

NECTARINES BAKED with ALMONDS and PISTACHIO NUTS

Fresh nectarines stuffed with a ground almond and chopped pistachio nut filling, baked in a clay pot until meltingly tender, then served with a passion fruit sauce.

SERVES 4

50g/2oz/½ cup ground almonds
15ml/1 tbsp caster (superfine) sugar
1 egg yolk
50g/2oz/⅓ cup shelled pistachio
   nuts, chopped
4 nectarines
200ml/7fl oz/scant 1 cup orange juice
2 ripe passion fruits
45ml/3 tbsp Cointreau or other
   orange liqueur

1 Soak a small clay pot, if using, in cold water for 15 minutes. Mix the ground almonds, sugar and egg yolk to a paste, then stir in the pistachio nuts.

2 Cut the nectarines in half and carefully remove the stones (pits). Pile the ground almond and pistachio filling into the nectarine halves and then place them in a single layer in the base of the clay pot or cazuela.

3 Pour the orange juice around the nectarines, then cover the pot or dish and place in an unheated oven. Set the oven to 200°C/400°F/Gas 6 and cook for 15 minutes.

4 Remove the lid from the pot or dish and bake for a further 5–10 minutes, or until the nectarines are soft. Transfer the nectarines to individual, warmed serving plates and keep warm.

5 Cut the passion fruits in half, scoop out the seeds and stir into the cooking juices in the clay pot or dish with the liqueur. Spoon the sauce around the nectarines and serve.

HONEY-BAKED FIGS with HAZELNUT ICE CREAM

This is a delectable dessert – fresh figs are baked in a lightly spiced lemon and honey syrup and served with a gorgeous, home-made roasted hazelnut ice cream.

SERVES 4

1 lemon grass stalk, finely chopped
1 cinnamon stick, roughly broken
60ml/4 tbsp clear honey
200ml/7fl oz/scant 1 cup water
8 large figs

For the hazelnut ice cream
450ml/¾ pint/scant 2 cups double
    (heavy) cream
50g/2oz/¼ cup caster (superfine) sugar
3 egg yolks
1.5ml/¼ tsp vanilla essence (extract)
75g/3oz/¾ cup hazelnuts

1 To make the ice cream, place the cream in a pan and heat slowly until almost boiling. Place the sugar and egg yolks in a bowl and beat until creamy.

2 Pour a little of the cream on to the egg yolk mixture and stir. Pour into the pan and mix with the rest of the cream. Cook over a low heat, stirring constantly, until the mixture thickens slightly and lightly coats the back of the spoon – do not allow it to boil. Pour into a bowl, then stir in the vanilla and leave to cool.

3 Preheat the oven to 180°C/350°F/ Gas 4. Place the hazelnuts on a baking sheet and roast for 10–12 minutes, or until golden. Leave the nuts to cool, then place them in a food processor or blender and process until they are coarsely ground.

4 Transfer the ice cream mixture to a metal or plastic freezer container and freeze for 2 hours, or until the mixture feels firm around the edge. Remove the container from the freezer and whisk the ice cream to break down the ice crystals. Stir in the ground hazelnuts and freeze the mixture again until half-frozen. Whisk again, then freeze until firm.

COOK'S TIPS
• If you prefer, rather than whisking the semi-frozen ice cream, tip it into a food processor and process until smooth.
• There are several different types of figs available and they can all be used in this recipe. Choose from green-skinned figs that have an amber-coloured flesh, dark purple-skinned fruit with a deep red flesh or green/yellow-skinned figs with a pinky-coloured flesh.

5 Place the lemon grass, cinnamon stick, honey and water in a small pan and heat slowly until boiling. Simmer the mixture for 5 minutes, then leave the syrup to stand for 15 minutes.

6 Meanwhile, soak a small clay pot in cold water for 15 minutes. Cut the figs into quarters, leaving them intact at the bases. Place the figs in the clay pot and pour over the honey-flavoured syrup.

7 Cover the clay pot and place in an unheated oven. Set the oven to 200°C/ 400°F/Gas 6 and bake the figs for about 15 minutes, or until tender.

8 Take the ice cream from the freezer about 10 minutes before serving, to soften slightly. Transfer the figs to serving plates. Strain a little of the cooking liquid over the figs and then serve them with a scoop or two of hazelnut ice cream.

VARIATION
This recipe also works well with halved, stoned (pitted) nectarines or peaches – simply cook as from step 6 and serve with the home-made ice cream.

STRAWBERRY OAT CRUNCH

This simple dessert looks good and tastes delicious. The strawberries form a tasty filling between the layers of oat crumble.

SERVES 4

150g/5oz/1¼ cups rolled oats
50g/2oz/½ cup wholemeal
   (whole-wheat) flour
75g/3oz/6 tbsp butter
30ml/2 tbsp pear and apple concentrate
500g/1¼lb strawberries
10ml/2 tsp arrowroot
natural (plain) yogurt, custard or cream,
   to serve

VARIATIONS
• Use dried apricots (chop half and cook the rest to a purée with a little apple juice) instead of the strawberries.
• Add a few chopped almonds or walnuts to the crumble mixture.

COOK'S TIP
You'll find pear and apple concentrate in good health food stores.

1 Preheat the oven to 180°C/350°F/ Gas 4. Mix the oats and flour in a bowl. Melt the butter with the apple and pear concentrate in a pan; stir into the bowl.

2 Purée half the strawberries in a food processor; chop the rest. Mix the arrowroot with a little of the strawberry purée in a small pan, then add the rest of the purée. Heat gently until thickened, then stir in the chopped strawberries.

3 Spread half the crumble mixture over the base of a shallow 18cm/7in round ovenproof earthenware dish to form a layer at least 1cm/½in thick. Top the crumble with the chopped and puréed strawberry mixture, then add the remaining crumble mixture, patting it down gently to form an even layer. Bake the oat crunch for about 30 minutes until golden brown. Serve warm or cold, with yogurt, custard or cream.

FRESH CURRANT BREAD and BUTTER PUDDING

Fresh mixed red- and blackcurrants add a tart touch to this scrumptious hot pudding in which layers of custard-soaked bread are cooked to a crisp golden crust.

SERVES 6

8 medium-thick slices day-old white bread,
   crusts removed
50g/2oz/¼ cup butter, softened
115g/4oz/1 cup redcurrants
115g/4oz/1 cup blackcurrants
4 eggs, beaten
75g/3oz/6 tbsp caster (superfine) sugar
475ml/16fl oz/2 cups creamy milk
5ml/1 tsp vanilla essence (extract)
freshly grated nutmeg
30ml/2 tbsp demerara (raw) sugar
single (light) cream, to serve

1 Preheat the oven to 160°C/325°F/
Gas 3. Butter a 1.2 litre/2 pint/5 cup
ovenproof earthenware dish.

VARIATION
A mixture of blueberries and raspberries
would work just as well as the currants.

2 Spread the slices of bread generously
with the butter, then cut them in half
diagonally. Layer the slices in the dish,
buttered side up, sprinkling the currants
between the layers.

3 Beat the eggs and caster sugar lightly
together in a large mixing bowl, then
gradually whisk in the creamy milk and
vanilla essence along with a large pinch
of freshly grated nutmeg.

4 Pour the milk mixture over the bread,
pushing the slices down into the liquid.
Sprinkle the demerara sugar and a little
more nutmeg over the top. Place the
dish in a roasting pan and fill with hot
water to come halfway up the sides of
the dish. Bake for 40 minutes, then
increase the oven temperature to
180°C/350°F/Gas 4 and bake for about
20 minutes more, or until the top is
golden. Serve warm, with single cream.

BAKED MAPLE and PECAN CROISSANT PUDDING

This variation of the classic English bread and butter pudding uses croissants, which give a light fluffy texture. Pecans, brandy-laced sultanas and maple-syrup-flavoured custard complete this mouthwatering dessert.

SERVES 4

75g/3oz/generous ½ cup sultanas
   (golden raisins)
45ml/3 tbsp brandy
50g/2oz/¼ cup butter, plus extra for greasing
4 large croissants
40g/1½oz/⅓ cup pecan nuts,
   roughly chopped
3 eggs, lightly beaten
300ml/½ pint/1¼ cups milk
150ml/¼ pint/⅔ cup single (light) cream
120ml/4fl oz/½ cup maple syrup
25g/1oz/2 tbsp demerara (raw) sugar
maple syrup and pouring (half-and-half)
   cream, to serve (optional)

1 Place the sultanas and brandy in a small pan and heat gently, until warm. Leave to stand for 1 hour. Soak a small clay pot in cold water for 15 minutes, then drain, leave for 2–3 minutes and lightly grease the base and sides.

2 Cut the croissants (see Cook's Tip) into thick slices, then spread with butter on one side.

3 Arrange the croissant slices, butter-side uppermost and slightly overlapping in the soaked clay pot. Sprinkle the brandy-soaked sultanas and the roughly chopped pecan nuts over the buttered croissant slices.

4 In a large bowl, beat the eggs and milk together, then gradually beat in the single cream and maple syrup.

5 Pour the egg custard through a sieve, over the croissants, fruit and nuts in the dish. Leave the uncooked pudding to stand for 30 minutes, so that some of the egg custard liquid is absorbed by the croissants.

6 Sprinkle the demerara sugar evenly over the top, then cover the dish and place in an unheated oven. Set the oven to 180°C/350°F/Gas 4 and bake for 40 minutes. Remove the lid and continue to cook for about 20 minutes, or until the custard is set and the top is golden.

7 Leave the pudding to cool for about 15 minutes before serving warm with extra maple syrup and a little pouring cream, if you like.

COOK'S TIPS
• This dessert is perfect for using up leftover croissants. Slightly stale one-day-old croissants are easier to slice and butter; they also soak up the custard more easily. Thickly sliced one-day-old bread or large slices of brioche could be used instead.
• Pecan nuts are an elongated nut in a glossy red oval-shaped shell, but are usually sold shelled. They are native to the USA and have a sweet, mild flavour. Pecans are most commonly used in pecan pie but are also popular in ice creams and cakes. Walnuts can be substituted for pecans in most recipes, and they would be perfect in this one if you don't have any pecan nuts.

INDEX